Revolution in writing

British literary responses to the French Revolution

Edited by Kelvin Everest

Open University Press
Milton Keynes · Philadelphia

Ideas and Production is published by
Open University Press in collaboration with
Anglia Polytechnic

Open University Press
Celtic Court, 22 Ballmoor
Buckingham MK18 1XW

and
1900 Frost Road, Suite 101
Bristol, PA 19007, USA

First published 1991

British Library Cataloguing in Publication Data

Revolution in writing: British literary responses to the French
Revolution. – (Ideas and production)
  I. Everest, Kelvin. II. Series
  820.94404

  ISBN 0–335–09756–1

Library of Congress Cataloging-in-Publication Data

Revolution in writing: British literary responses to the French
  Revolution/edited by Kelvin Everest.
      p.   cm. – (Ideas and production)
  Includes index.
  ISBN 0–335–09756–1
  1. Revolutionary literature, English – History and criticism.
  2. France – History – Revolution, 1789–1799 – Literature and the
  revolution.   3. English literature – 18th century – History and
  criticism.   4. English literature – 19th century – History and
  criticism.   5. France – History – Revolution, 1789–1799 – Influence.
  6. English literature – French influences.   7. Romanticism – Great
  Britain. I. Everest, Kelvin. II. Series.
  PR129.F8R48   1991
  820.9'358 – dc20   91-23865   CIP

Typeset by Type Study, Scarborough
Printed in Great Britain by St Edmundsbury Press,
Bury St Edmunds, Suffolk

Contents

Contributors

Kelvin Everest is A.C. Bradley Professor of Modern Literature at the University of Liverpool. He has published widely on the literature of the Romantic period.

Tom Furniss is a Lecturer in the Department of English Studies at the University of Strathclyde. He has published a number of articles on the Revolution Controversy and on Edmund Burke's aesthetics and is currently writing a book on Burke.

Harriet Devine Jump is a Lecturer in English at Edge Hill College, Lancashire. She has published articles on Wordsworth, Coleridge and Akenside, and is editor of, and contributor to, *Diverse Voices: Twentieth-Century Women's Writing from Around the World* (Harvester Wheatsheaf, 1991). She is currently working on a book on Mary Wollstonecraft for Harvester Wheatsheaf's Key Critics series.

Philip W. Martin has taught at Exeter University, King Alfred's College, Winchester, and Cheltenham and Gloucester College of Higher Education. He is the author of *Byron: A Poet before his Public* (1982), *Mad Women in Romantic Writing* (1987), joint editor of *Reviewing Romanticism* (forthcoming) and joint British editor of the journal *Literature and History*. He is a founder member of the British Association for Romantic Studies, and joint editor of its bulletin.

Michael Rossington is a Lecturer in Literature at The Open University and is currently engaged in preparing his thesis on Shelley and mythology for publication, and preparing *The Cenci* for the forthcoming Longman edition of *The Poems of Shelley*, volume two, edited by Kelvin Everest.

Kathryn Sutherland is a Lecturer in English at the University of Manchester. She has published articles on Scott, Wordsworth, and Lamb, amongst other topics. She is currently writing a book on women and the institution of history in the eighteenth century.

John Whale is a Lecturer in English at the University of Leeds. He is the author of *Thomas De Quincey's Reluctant Autobiography* (1984) and a number of articles on Burke, De Quincey, Hazlitt, and Wollstonecraft. With Stephen Copley he has co-edited a volume of essays which reassesses the literature of the Romantic period and is currently completing a book on the relationship between aesthetics and politics in the same period entitled *Imagination Under Pressure*.

Cover illustration by Ed d'Souza, cover design by Will Hill.

Text illustrations

Patrick Preston	2
Andrew Gregory	8
Hazel Hare	28
Selina Young	64
Neil Evans	102
Mark Hatenboer	120
Andrew Webster	138, 157

Art Editor: Will Hill

Acknowledgements

The editors acknowledge the help of the following who have assisted in the production of *Revolution in Writing: British Literary Responses to the French Revolution*: Mike Salmon, Tom Allcock, Steve Marshall of Anglia Polytechnic, Cambridge, and John Skelton, Ray Cunningham and Sue Hadden of the Open University Press for their material support in establishing Ideas and Production as a Series; Ian Gordon, Head of the Department of Arts and Letters, Anglia Polytechnic, for his consistent support for the project; Kate Campbell for copy editing; the Computer Centre, and Division of Graphic Reproduction and Printing, Anglia Polytechnic, for invaluable help in the production process, particularly Clive Bray, Nicky Morland, Colin Wood and the BTEC HND Illustration students and course administrators. A particular thanks is due to Nora Crook, for her expert's index.

1

Introduction

Kelvin Everest

The essays collected in this volume were all originally generated by the academic conferences and events organised throughout Britain to mark the two hundredth anniversary of the French Revolution. These conferences in 1989 were diverse in their style, thematic organisation, and scale but they shared an energy and enthusiasm which testified vividly to the vitality of Romantic studies in this country. The main conferences took place in Winchester at King Alfred's College, and at the Universities of Leicester, Lancaster and Leeds. There was also a conference on related topics at Glasgow University early in 1990, which represented a continuation and development of themes that had emerged in 1989.

Discussion at these conferences was always lively, always diverse in its positions and perspectives, and dominated by a pleasingly constructive and friendly atmosphere. This atmosphere embraced scholars from different disciplines, different kinds of educational institution and indeed different countries (North American participation was particularly high). Many of the participants were young, or at least at a relatively early stage in their academic careers. The papers which make up the present volume are all by younger academics. This relative youth, combined with the friendliness, variety and intellectual vigour of the conferences, produced a marked sense of celebration; a kind of measured delight in the intellectual contemplation of an historical event of such devastating complexity, richness and weight of implication.

Certain themes, inevitably, appeared again and again throughout the papers and debates, and those themes are reflected in the

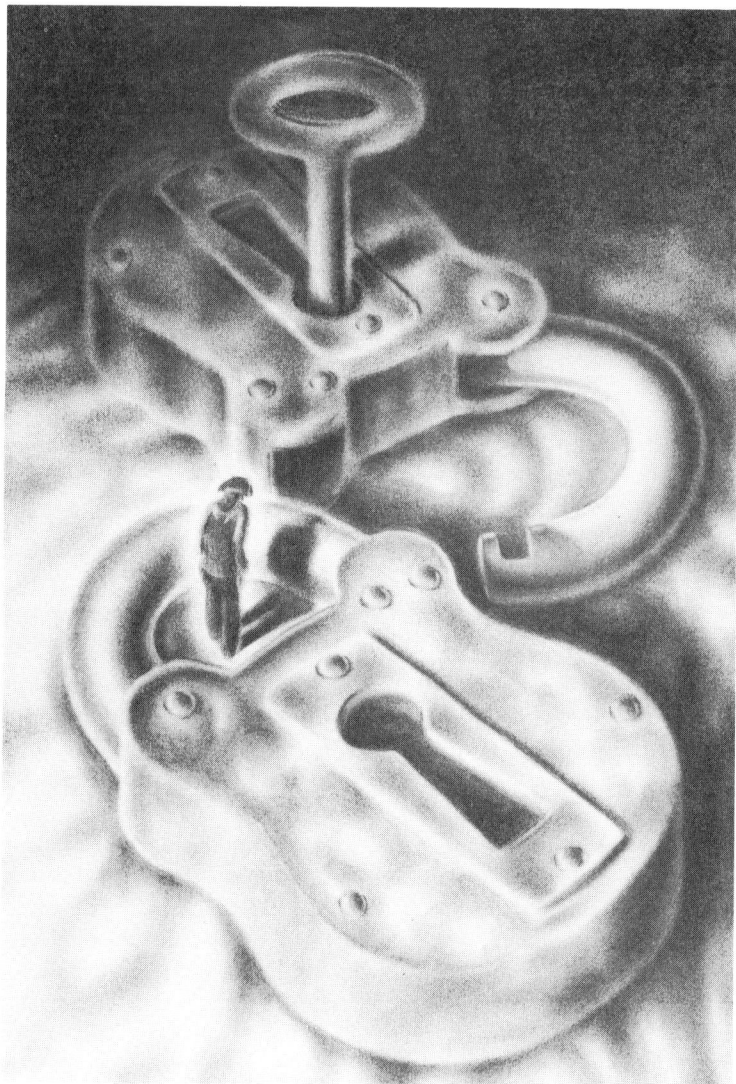

Patrick Preston

arguments of the essays that are collected here. At the centre of much debate, whether explicitly or implicitly, is a continually recurring problem: how, in our account of the past, its ideas and its art, are we to negotiate between texts, history and theory? This problem of negotiation is of course by now extremely familiar, indeed inescapable, in its taxing combination of self-reflexivity, instrumentality and politically charged polemic. Its most influential, or at least most controversial form in current debate is that of the 'new historicism', a mainly American theoretical idiom typified for Romantic studies in the work of Marjorie Levinson. Philip Martin's discussion, which opens this volume, addresses some striking features and problems of the new historicism, and offers a characterisation of its capacities and limitations. Those capacities are undeniably powerful in the hands of sophisticated practitioners. Professor Levinson's readings of Wordsworth and Keats, for example, accomplish a most searching and subtle engagement with the discursive formations into which we are ushered by Romantic poetry. Such engagements are defining of new historicist practice; what we are obliged to confront is the extent to which modes and goals of critical reading are functions of the texts under consideration. The new historicist project seeks a self-consciousness in reading which heightens awareness of this function in texts. The power of the text to shape the way we read it is countered by a heightened consciousness of those contemporary discursive formations which form our own modes and goals as critics, situated in our own, utterly different historical moment. We are urged to consciousness of the 'historicity' of the discourses addressed in critical reading, and thus to a properly critical awareness of the ideological nature of the world view predicated by Romanticism.

The preoccupation with discursive formations produces its own problems, however. Marxists in particular, but also critics in a broader British tradition of Left-radical social history and contextual literary-historical commentary, are doubtful about the real political efficacy of an interpretive mode which consigns all history to a function of the discursive configurations obtaining at the moment of interpretation. The new historicism appears in a fundamental sense post-structuralist, in its commitment to the idea of meaning as a product of synchronically existing signifying systems. History has no depth, and no form of material continuity; it is a purely mental construction. Paradoxically, this enables new historicist practice to credit texts from the past with great, even coercive power, because they can draw us into their own discursive formations and create the illusion of a real continuity between their historical moment and our own.

There are, needless to say, powerful alternative theoretical positions available, and Philip Martin shows that there are even virtually opposite positions. Tony Bennett, for example, argues persuasively for texts as 'strategic sites for the contestation of dominant subject identities' (see p. 25), so that, in Dr Martin's words, 'subjects [that is, readers, *users* of texts] are not interpellated by texts, but conduct an active interest in them, and that interest – in the broadest sense – is political'. Escape from the bewildering hall-of-mirrors effect of new historicist reading is arguable by such a route. The clash of discrete discursive formations which is necessarily involved in any reading of the past may yet be preserved for actual political purposes. But this has to be done by acknowledging the continuities which enable us to make sense of our radical difference from the past.

The reality of women's historical experience poses the political question sharply. There can be little advantage in thinking of our understanding of women's experience in the French Revolutionary period, for example, merely as the ghostly backward projection of present discursive formations. Such a position is at once to relativise, in a hopelessly compromising way, the moral grounds of present political commitment, and offensively to appropriate the actual experience of other people. The real complexity of women's emergence into conscious social identity, in the last years of the eighteenth century, and under the pressures of the dramatic revolutionary situation, can be immensely illuminating in the context of current social experience and the effort to understand it. Mary Wollstonecraft is obviously a crucial and central figure here, and her work and life form a major preoccupation in this volume, as they did throughout the bicentenary conferences.

And yet the studies which attend to her achievement here repeatedly return us to the paradoxes and entrapments of discursive formations. Wollstonecraft's ability to encounter and deal with the crises of her life and historical moment was limited and shaped by the styles of representation available to her. She, like the rest of us, was constrained to represent and account for her experience and ideas by the dominant representational and theoretical idioms of her community. The resultant strains and contradictions are intriguingly brought out and developed by several of the discussions in this volume. In particular, her efforts to elaborate a rationalist feminism, in the context of pro-revolutionary polemic, are constantly driven to embrace representations of the female governed by the assumptions of her opponents. A number of the essays collected here share a very specific concern with one particular site of contention in the debates of the Romantic period about the significance of events in France: the crisis of the 'October Days' of 5–6 October 1789, when the French royal family were threatened by a revolutionary mob at Versailles, and were subsequently removed to Paris together with the National Assembly. These events are given crucial prominence in Burke's account, and they therefore become crucial too for Wollstonecraft, and indeed for Paine. But they are more than simply a common site of interpretation. Interpretations of these events draw on fundamentally similar assumptions which eerily merge the positions of ostensibly opposed commentators.

This tendency to take on the guise of the enemy is exactly the danger about which the new historicism has succeeded in making us so vigilant, with respect to our general encounter with the texts of Romanticism. Romantic texts seek to constrain us to read as Romantics. Frequently, their internal structures mirror the external relations between text and reader: Caleb and Falkland, in Godwin's *Caleb Williams*, or Frankenstein and his monster in Mary Shelley's novel, provide archetypal instances of such structures, in their modelling of an antithetical relation whose ostensibly opposed terms mirror and feed upon each other.

But as readers we need not in practice simply succumb to the allure of such strategies. It remains possible to read against, as well as under, the influence of complex discursive formations. In feminist terms, for example, it is arrestingly demonstrated by Kathryn Sutherland's essay in this volume that the representations of our own cultural politics, just as those of Wollstonecraft's revolutionary politics, can be shown to elide and conceal still recoverable alternative representations. Thus the Christian conservatism of Hannah More's pamphlet propaganda emerges as more immediate and telling, in its address to real female experience in the 1790s, than the overt radical-rationalist feminism of Wollstonecraft's work, with its clear affinities with the characteristically left-wing feminist politics of our own epoch.

Kathryn Sutherland's essay demonstrates the power of history to surprise and confound our expectations; to tell us what we do not perhaps necessarily wish to hear, so to speak. The most powerful discursive formations are susceptible of fracture, and not only under the weight of internal contradiction. The past may emerge as altogether more various and unmanageable than any account can allow for. Harriet Devine Jump's essay on Wollstonecraft's *Historical and Moral View . . . of the French Revolution* shows how, in Wollstonecraft's own case, her direct observation of events in France in the early nineties served not to endorse, but worryingly to enter questions about the validity and the practical consequences of a theoretical position. Radicals in the revolutionary period found themselves compelled to elaborate an explanation for the wild and dangerous potentialities unleashed in a populace newly out of state control. History unfolded – at the level of event and reaction and counter-reaction from day to day – too quickly, too unpredictably. And this meant too that the intellectuals of revolution, its propheciers and schemers and advocates, found themselves suddenly unable to escape responsibility for terrible consequences which had been quite unforeseen, and indeed unforeseeable. The dilemma – anticipated in Wollstonecraft's dawning nervousness and uncertainty as an observer of the early revolutionary days – is brilliantly realised and dramatised in Shelley's representation of Beatrice Cenci, as Michael Rossington's essay demonstrates. Beatrice comes to stand as an image of the liberal intellectual whose idealism cannot in the end transcend the grim actuality of events which she has helped to set in train.

These reflections derive from the discussions carried on within and across the essays which follow. But they do not derive exclusively from them. The conference season of 1989 was exciting, and it takes its place in the memory now as the academic inflection of more general and more boisterous celebrations, involving the whole French nation and its admirers across the world. The excitement merged, as that year drew on, into far more momentous and moving excitements, with the extraordinary acceleration of political change in Eastern Europe, the collapse of the Berlin wall, the climactic Christmas revolution in Romania. Bliss was it . . .

It is tremendously hard to make an effective leap of historical imagination, and to try seriously to understand what the experiences of the early 1790s can actually have meant to contemporaries; what they can have meant, that is, absolutely without the foreknowledge of a Terror, of Napoleon, of a quarter-century of European conflict, without the whole agenda of post-Napoleonic international politics which was implicitly set over a few short months, and which took a century or more in the working out. But that leap of historical imagination has turned out a little easier for our generation than anyone could have anticipated. Once the political agenda is torn up, a lot can change in thirteen months.

Andrew Gregory

2

Romanticism, history, historicisms

Philip W. Martin

The new historicism, to some the latest and most spectacular *ignis fatuus* of critical movements, was rightly at the forefront of our thoughts during the French Revolution's bi-centenary. Rightly, because the historicity it is bent on affirming is that which centres the conceptualising of the past within the historically realised moment of the present. And since new historicism (without permission, so it seems) had pitched its mansion in a place fundamental to the current anatomy of Romanticism – that is, Wordsworth studies – there was sharp sensitivity to its claims. Yet despite a general alertness, there has also been a remarkable silence about new historicism in Romantic Studies, most readily evinced in Alan Liu's recent article in *ELH* (1989), wherein Liu, a Romanticist, argues volubly on the issue of new historicism in Renaissance studies, but says very little about its effects in the province of his own scholarship.

One of the most striking features of Romantic new historicism is that few self-conscious proponents exist. It is a belated labelling which structures the movement, and critics are interpellated into its folds. Marjorie Levinson is the central figure in this activity (hence this paper's concentration on her work) and her introduction to *Re-thinking Historicism* (and her essay therein) offers striking instances of this, as she hails her contributors and others in the name of the new methodology (Levinson *et al.* 1989). She conducted a similar roll-call at the beginning of her book on Wordsworth (Levinson 1986). Possibly many of the names invoked were oblivious of their practice as new or proto-historicists as they wrote, and yet this offers no difficulty to the historicising mind. For in its latest manifestation it sees historical

process not as a continuum, an accumulation of fixed forms or
events on a historical record, there to be reconstituted by archival
research. Rather, it sees history as of the present, in that so far as
it is a process, this process is a configuration of history or histories
constantly forming and reforming through the belated knowledge of the here and now. History has long been seen as existing
only in the moment of its realisation, but this is different, for the
emphasis is not on cognition as such but on what can be seen in
the past through the informed, or misinformed, slanted views of
the present, which has its own historicity. The new historicism is,
in a sense, a 'perpetual weaving and unweaving of ourselves'.

One large interference for new historicism within Romantic
studies is the work going on under that title in the Renaissance,
where it made its first establishment. There the new movement
declares itself against the old as exemplified in the work of
E.M.W. Tillyard, but Romanticism identifies its old historicism in
a very different politics, the work of E.P. Thompson or David
Erdman. This difference might be more striking in England than
America, so much more so that the theoretical commonality
might not be perceived. Where Tillyard asserts an ordered
stability of social context, Erdman and Thompson find one riven
with dispute and strife, reclaiming for their contemporary
readers submerged class interest and repressed cultures. While it
may be the case that Tillyard and Thompson share a very broad
methodological base (Hegelian, Zeitgeist, a history wherein
cultural artefacts such as literary texts reflect, express or provide
analogues of an essential social history) I believe it is new
historicism's constant liability to forget its effects by being
absorbed in its methods, to underestimate political difference
and the varied purpose of old historicist analysis in its haste to
declare its new coherence against the methods of the past. This
political confusion – or at least its impending presence – is
something to which I will return at the end of this paper.

Romantic new historicism then, is distinct from Renaissance
new historicism partly because of the difference of its difference.
It is perhaps more mindful of its predicates in the history of the
left, and it moves out from these bases to conduct its new project.
Broadly, that old historicist ambition was archival and contextualising, the uncovering of a historical record into which texts
fitted so that their meanings could be fixed. Such contextual work
continues within that variety of writing that Marjorie Levinson
has ushered into the new historicist fold, so much so that this

new movement is not consistently visible against the old. It is also the case, as Jon Klancher has pointed out (1989), that Romantic new historicism is far closer to cultural materialism (although I believe similar confusions have been made in Renaissance studies by conflating Greenblatt and Dollimore). Nevertheless, it is clear that Levinson perceives a difference, and it remains to be explained what, in the terms of this new methodology, was wrong with the old.

Clearly one ought to begin with Althusser and then move on through the post-structuralisms generally, but there is not room here for such a totalising explanation. Contextualising as a method is what is at stake, and this will provide my focus. It is, of course, an awkward methodological act, since its tendency is undialectical, one-sided, to situate a text in what often turn out to be complex webs of ideological and institutional influence, or simply other discourses, without situating the critic or historian who conducts this exercise in the present. At least that remains invisible, and the lack of awareness, if not the lack of problematisation, leads to an overdetermined text and the illusion of an underdetermined subject (the critic) producing that text and its overdeterminations within what appears to be an authoritative materiality – history, real events. Contextualisation tends towards the idea of an objective history, an unproblematised view of the past. In its most general sense there is nothing wrong with this, for most loosely, history might be conceived of as a series of events, a chronology of wars, revolutions, acts of parliament. In order to cement such events in place, the historian produces documents as evidence. But immediately the documents are organised, read or even interpreted, history becomes a text. Equally, immediately it becomes anything more than the most primitive of chronological tables, it becomes a narrative. Even so, most of us can live with this without too much agonising, since the problems thus created are only the problems of textuality, which *in themselves* are not so great, once deference to them has been made. A far greater difficulty here exists in the types of history that might provide the context: will it be for example material/documentary history, ideological history, intellectual history? The problem is a pragmatic one: texts can be made to seek out an intellectual history, or an ideological one, yet such a history suffers within the double bind of being positivist or non-material, since it cannot be empirically based, in the same way as documentary history, the history of legislation, laundry bills, birth and death certificates. As a consequence, as LaCapra has noted, it is generally assumed that the 'only significant historical questions are those that can be answered by empirical (preferably archival) research'(1985: 19), and given the tyranny of this empiricism and the narrow boundaries it imposes, the materialist context is always going to be restricted. LaCapra rightly states that this kind of context frequently goes under the name of 'historical reality.' As a result,

> the notion of context may even serve in some way to get around texts and the problem of interpreting or reading them other than in reductively documentary ways. A wedge is driven between history and critical theory.
>
> (LaCapra 1985: 38)

By critical theory I take it LaCapra is referring to the production of meanings within a newly problematised methodology; broadly, the seeking out of the connotative rather than denotative, the reading of texts against the grain, and of course, what he calls 'the textual dimensions of documents themselves'. He is surely right and thus explains the contemporary conflict – familiar to all of us shuttling between departments or trying to work in inter-disciplinary ways – between historians and critics. Hermeneutics is too often inimical to a historical method that puts its faith in the reading of documents.

Hayden White sees the text-context relationship as a crucial one, and raises the critically awkward questions that those of us accustomed to the old methods have to face:

> What is this relationship? What, indeed, is a text – an entity that once had an assuring solidity and concreteness, indeed a kind of identity that allowed it to serve as a model of whatever was comprehensible in both culture and nature. What happened to that text that used to lay before the scholar in a comforting materiality and possessed an auth-ority that the 'context' in which it had arisen and to the existence of which it attested could never have? Where is this context which literary historians used to invoke as a matter of course to 'explain' the distinctive features of the poetic text and to anchor it in an ambience more solid than words? What are the dimensions and levels of this context? Where does it begin and end? And what is its status as a component of the historically real which it is the historian's purpose to identify if not to explain? The text-context relationship, once an

unexamined presupposition of historical investigation, has
become a problem.

(White 1987: 186)

Indeed this is the case. Given that 'context' (as its etymology
indicates) is inflected by the text, then it partakes of its rhetoric.
Further, as the text is being produced in the act of reading, then
the critic-reader-historian needs to be situated – or at least
declared as a presence – in this process of making history.
LaCapra uses the psychoanalytical term 'transference' to refer to
this, suggesting that a dialogical relationship with the past can be
constructed if one is conscious of transference as a 'repetition/
displacement of the "object" of study in one's own discourse
about it', and the argument here strongly suggests that it is the
repression of this knowledge that allows the delusion of a full
identification with the past (empathy) and the notion of its
objective representation. Hayden White enacts much the same
confrontation with objective history, preferring a linguistic
model to a psychoanalytical one, arguing that old historicism
presupposes a naturalised notion of language and the world it
represents (1987: 198). Thus texts are made to 'represent' the
world: as a symptom or effect of causal relations (the old Marxist
model); as a formal manifestation of a given culture (philology);
as an analogical representation of a culture (Hegelian-Zeitgeist
theory). All methods perhaps, turn texts into documents, insist
that they are representational of the world they once inhabited,
which is still there, as it were, *within* the text for the purpose of
reconstruction. Texts run the risk of being read as synecdoches of
history if their contexts are constantly being made for them so
that they may be understood. White's way out of this is by way of
Saussure and what he takes as post-structuralist linguistic
theory, which will see the text as that 'which will bear no
necessary, or "motivated" relation to that which it signifies'. In
other words, we cannot suppose an unmediated relation between signs and the world, between texts and history. By seeing
the text semiologically however, White – like LaCapra – transfers
attention to the production of meanings. The centre of interest is
now the text's codes, in a way then, its formal properties,
considered as 'a dynamic process of overt and covert code
shifting by which a specific subjectivity is called up and established in the reader, who is supposed to entertain this representation of the world as a realistic one in virtue of its congeniality to

the imaginary relationship the subject bears to his [sic] own social and cultural situation' (White 1987: 193). Here the text becomes a resource for the production of meanings: studying its codes is a way of seeing history internalised within the text, a way of providing insight into the kind of 'meaning production' available at a given historical moment. Thus (of course) texts change meanings as they move through history, and we are left with an alternative: to study the history of meanings (literary historiography) or to reconstitute formalism by moving into semiological readings.

My preference would be for the former, in effect, the study of reading formations. How then, in trying to construct these formations of the past do we situate ourselves in relation to the Romantic period, and in relation to what we take as its history? Context has long been a problematic fascination for Romanticists, and much relatively recent work (perhaps from *Natural Supernaturalism* onwards) has been concerned with making meaning contingent upon context: certain meanings, topical allusions, only come to light through historical investigation, and this kind of research activity is perhaps most characteristic of the cultural-materialist approach of many British scholars; Marilyn Butler's books, Heather Glen's work on Blake and Wordsworth (1983), Nigel Leask's uncovering and elaboration of Coleridge's place in a tradition of agrarian republicanism (1988), Olivia Smith's subtle recompositions of the political meanings inherent in Romantic language (1984). But this contextual work, which would include in my opinion Marjorie Levinson's book on Wordsworth, whether materialist or Machereyan in tendency, whether archetypal and Hegelian or local and lexical in character (explanatory in terms of locating the historical lexicon) was and is ever vulnerable to critiques based on refutations of immanent meanings. Quite apart from the liability of intentionalism and the restitution of a *cogito*, an individual rather than a *subject*, and apart too from the unregarded provisionality of historical knowledge masquerading as finite and beyond disruption, which in its extremity, such criticism might portend, this style of contextualising, it is argued, moves towards an objectified past against which signification is transfixed. As a method without a political cause – and here I am conscious that a number of the examples listed above have one – contextualisation proposes a totalised past into which the causes of the present might only make an illegitimate entry. That suggestion of the historical factor as a guarantee of transcending meaning is, in its most reducible form, a vital opposition to the post-structuralist questioning of factors existing outside of writing and determining it. The real problem of course is one of demarcation – context as something convertible to a currency or quantity 'outside writing.' Once it is admitted that there can only be a history of writing (whether this be Derrida's *écriture* or something more literal) and that discourses act and react continuously upon and within each other, contemporaneously or across time, then the prospect of history as the shaping or transfixing backcloth for the signifier has to be surrendered, and we are left with an agglomeration of troping which denies historical sequence as we once knew it (*pace* Harold Bloom) or the shifting sands of meaning that must underlie the discourse formations *we* construct, since their arrangements are always only relative to each other.

This is a summary of the theoretical crisis that new historicism is prepared to confront and, confronting it, find an alternative mode of study to that offered by Yale deconstruction. Yet one wonders whether the crisis is properly confronted and solved, and further, whether it existed forcibly in practice in the first place. I will deal briefly with the latter issue first. Historical readings, in practice, have rarely been conducted within a hard-line Hegelian or Marxist mode. History, or historical process, is seldom 'read off' against texts synecdochally. Rather, following Thompson, cultural materialists working within Romanticism have recovered, and are still recovering, repressed cultures. In other words a context is being reclaimed for writers which they were previously denied: work on Blake throws up the obvious examples; he has been put back in Lambeth having been removed, most ironically, to the academy. Such readings have not been conducted from a proclaimed disinterestedness. These are politicising works: the reading formations of recent decades, more fully democratised in terms of social class than those of the past, have an interest in discovering the politics and class relations of Romantic texts, of enquiring into their relations with the radical cultures of their time. This kind of curiosity has led to historicist investigation in the sense that matters of material production (for example, readership, public, topical allusion) have been seen as bearing directly – causally – on the making of texts. But to say as much, as Jameson points out so eloquently in *The Political Unconscious*, is not to defer utterly to the doctrine of mechanical causality: it is simply to note that texts are socially produced (1981: 25–28). An act of political reclamation therefore, in the form of a cultural-materialist re-reading, is an interested investigation of the past from the politically determined view of the present. As such it partakes of the self-consciousness which new historicism requires, and further, it does not necessarily imply the existence of an objective or totalising history.

Yet of course there is a major difference, although as I see it that difference is not fully worked out. New historicism, so nervous of the grand narrative of history, defers to Foucauldian rather than Marxist versions of history. Even so this can be seen as an opposition about which – in Romantic studies at least – it is nervous, for in the writings of Marjorie Levinson, Marx is a far greater presence than Foucault. Nevertheless, new historicism is determined to be rid of a teleology, and is therefore happier with Foucault's *epistemes* than Marx's dialectical materialism; happier, also, with localised archaeologies rather than with what it must be regarding as ideal history. Its major difficulty is that in ridding itself of the historical continuum, it is compelled to situate the present in an alternative way. What interest does new historicism have in the past? How will it site itself in relation to that past? In its latest manifestations, its prime mover seemingly is its self-consciousness, its almost ironic awareness that it is caught up within the myths and the modes of discourse that it is examining. If the precursive or proto-new historicist opening move within Romanticism was McGann's *Romantic Ideology*, which struggled to locate a position outside the precincts of Romantic values to permit a proper critique, then the developed position is that argued in Marjorie Levinson's essay 'Back to the Future' where she states:

> To ask these questions is to insist that we re-write the past with the full complement of contemporary knowledges. It is also to name ourselves as producers of the past as past and thus of history's meaning, even as we bring out the historical overdetermination of our productive acts and even as we renounce a fully dialectical knowledge of ourselves. We define ourselves as a potential structure to be actualised by whatever generation it is that turns around and seeks us out as its way of living its present.
>
> (Levinson *et al.* 1989: 52)

Clifford Siskin, in *The Historicity of Romantic Discourse*, fulfils a similar project by resolutely turning aside from the 'developmental tale' of literary history (which he identifies as a Romantic act) to move within what he calls a generic history which avoids absolute classification systems. He use genre to construct a history, rather than supposing that there is such a thing as the teleology of (say) the novel. Thus a form might be entered into hierarchical relations with other forms at a given historical moment, but the criticism which is willing to articulate this is also interrelational with other forms. That Romantic criticism is repeatedly enacting Romantic gestures (growth, organicism, individualism, development) is in a way the position from which he begins and with which he ends, so while noting the non-self-conscious rehearsal of such gestures, he admits the constraints of his own discourse and operates self-consciously, not supposing that an objectified release from the bounds of Romantic discourse is easily achieved. It is not simply a matter of will. His historicising is a historiography of Romantic criticism which is concerned to show how the configuration of a 'psychologised self' is made both within Romanticism and ineluctably, by the reading formations structured by modes of criticism, whose operations can themselves be configured by descriptions of institutional power. The Romantic self therefore, while ubiquitous, is also shown as culture-specific. Nevertheless, there is a strong awareness here of the ways in which the past may determine the interests of the present.

New historicism's major contribution has been in its questioning of the constructing of a relationship to the past, and in particular in its identifications of how the relationships inherited from other forms of criticism are built around paradigms which are in themselves Romantic. Its heightened consciousness about the cultural determinants of critical practice, however, make it particularly nervous about articulating its critical interest. Since there is no objective past, then how can there be an objective present? Since we can trace the gaps in the past's knowledge about itself by way of our own slanted present, how can we see the gaps that are informing our own critical procedure? If the past is caught in webs of power relations, how can we suppose that we are free spirits? These are the kinds of questions clustering on the edge of new historicist practice, and because of the way they pull away from empiricism, because of their dwelling on indeterminacy and provisional knowledge, it is pertinent to enquire into new historicism's understanding of empiricism and material history.

The context offered by the new historicist is not so much that of a series of circumstances and events that explain the text's allusions, but more probably, that which elucidates the text's silences and repressions. Context doesn't add up to a background, fixed and still to be found in place if we suddenly discovered that our text were an hallucination and disappeared. No, if that were the case the context would vanish too, since it is dependent on an ordering of extra-textual discourses and cultural events according to the problematics of specific textual aporias. So, to what extent is the new historicism an empirical discipline? Levinson argues forcefully that it is, but in order to veer away from enlightenment history, a history of mechanical causality or grand narratives, she proposes an awkward formula:

> Ours is an empirically responsible investigation of the contemporary meanings informing literary works . . . as well as other social texts. We regard these meanings as systematically interrelated within the period in question, but since we do not organise the system by a dynamic concept of ideology on the one hand, and of structural determination on the other, our enquiries do not give rise to a meaningful historical sequence. In the absence of some such model of epochal relatedness, questions concerning our own critical interest cannot materialise . . .
>
> (Levinson *et al.* 1989: 20)

The empiricism apparently inheres in the belief that art is *socially* produced (at its inception and at the moments of its reproductions) but this familiar model is not to be organised by a working concept of ideology or sequences of causal relations: it is as if new historicism begins with an old historicist project of restoring voices to the dead, but is then interrupted by the spectre of Foucault, or more likely that of Clifford Geertz, the cultural anthropologist who has had a major influence on the Renaissance new historicists. As 'questions concerning our own critical interest cannot materialise' the provisional nature of the present interest is all that can be articulated, and this is achieved by reliance on a model of there being a symbiotic relationship between the critic and history:

> it is precisely our interest in the Romantic ideology – I shall say, its interest in us . . .

> Today's criticism differs in its untheorised and unself-consciously political situation. This gives it a special place – a

place privileged, ironically, by the kind and extent of its possession by the object it studies . . .

We are the ones who, by putting the past to a certain use, put it in a certain order. While most of us know this, we seem not to consider that this interest of ours in a certain use might also be an *effect* of the past which we study . . .

(Levinson *et al.* 1989: 18, 19, 21)

In her formulations the critical act is determined by its object of study: while she wants to retain what she calls 'specifically Marxian critical methods and values', she rejects what she takes to be the self-determining notion of politicising a text, wilfully, as it were, referring to this as 'use-value pragmatism' which

imagines a work capable of dissolving the traces of its production and its history of receptions. The proposition that we can in any simple sense 'make a poem's politics for it' is also a definition of a text which descends – or rather ascends – to us in a pure form.

(Levinson *et al.* 1989: 21)

And yet Levinson insists that the new historicism will 'situate politics within the work and typically, at the level of its allusive structure' – the object of the study is representation, representational acts, and politics in the historicist coinage, refers to 'the real', 'actual circumstances and their apparent inter-relations, as well as the covert logic obtaining among these data in the contemporary mind.' In studying the representation of the real (as Levinson's work on Wordsworth indicates) there is a highly specific gathering of information which will then, having partly explained the text's allusions and elidings, situate its ideological position. But position, as Levinson admits, is static: this is a synchronically perceived web of interrelations because 'historicists do not . . . generally assume the ongoing proliferation of positions by a contradiction-engendering base of any kind.' (1989: 56)

I am taking these quotations from a lengthy footnote to the essay 'Back to the Future' and I think they explain why Levinson says that the new historicist 'embrace of the Marxian methodology is a delicately sensitive affair.' This selection might be seen as an eradication, for Marxism without the contradiction-engendering base of class conflict might as well be called nothing at all. But Levinson is not explicit about this: what she is turning to is a model of cultural representation that is localising discursive acts within what I will call (following Tony Bennett 1983 and 1987) reading formations – these formations being constructed vertically in the symbiotic model (critic-history) of which Levinson is so fond, or laterally as what is taken to be the text's claim upon its referents. New historicism will attempt to conceive of these together of course, in a self-reflexive act that confesses the impossibility of objectivity. Nevertheless, this localising effectively gives to discourse a peculiarly independent life; representation – in one sense – becomes the only form of access to the real which then becomes highly fragmented and highly specific. This is surely where Geertz comes in. Levinson does not quote Geertz, but he is an acknowledged influence behind Renaissance new historicism, and in a now famous passage negotiates his way round old historicism (he has Marx and Hegel in mind) as follows:

> In order to avoid having to regard ideas, concepts, values, and expressive forms either as shadows cast by the organis-ation of society upon the hard surfaces of history or as the soul of history whose progress is but a working out of their internal dialectic, it has proved necessary to regard them as independent but not self-sufficient forces – as acting and having their impact only within specific social contexts to which they have, to a greater or lesser degree, a determining influence.
>
> (Geertz 1975: 361)

According to Geertz, cultural analysis must be undertaken through ethnography, which in its enquiries is confronted by 'a multiplicity of complex conceptual structures, many of them superimposed upon or knotted into one another, which are at once strange, irregular and inexplicit, and which [one] must contrive somehow first to grasp and then to render.' This is Geertz's method of thick description – a 'sorting out [of] the structures of signification' which involves the recognition that what is 'called data' is really 'our own constructions of other people's constructions of what they and their compatriots are up to . . .' (1975: 9–10). The parallels with new historicism's obsessive subject-object relations are striking, and Geertz himself likens what he is doing in cultural anthropology to literary criticism, yet there is another aspect of Geertz's work which, whether directly influential in new historicist practice or merely operating in parallel, helps to explain what it is doing. Geertz claims that culture is neither 'objective' nor 'subjective' but operational. It performs no psychological role and is not held in the minds of men. In other words he creates the field of the 'ideational' as a field of action, and wrests it entirely away from concepts of ideology:

> Culture, this acted document, thus is public, like a bur-lesqued wink or a mock sheep raid. Though ideational, it does not exist in someone's head; though unphysical, it is not an occult entity . . . Once human behaviour is seen as symbolic action – action which . . . signifies – the question as to whether culture is patterned conduct or a frame of mind, or even the two somehow mixed together, loses sense. The thing to ask about a burlesqued wink or a mock sheep raid is not what their ontological status is . . . – they are things of this world. The thing to ask is what their import is: what it is . . . that is getting said.
>
> (Geertz 1975: 10)

This subversion of the concept of ideology and reliance on 'thick description' as a study of communication might lead us to a better understanding of what might be called new historicism's func-tionalism, a functionalism which is preoccupied with *configur-ations* above all else, layers of coding and encoding which include those of the analyst. What is privileged is the performative.

This brings me back to the questions which 'cannot material-ise', questions about the nature of current critical interest. By situating the critic firmly and absolutely in the present, from which there is conducted an ethnological excursion through thick descriptions into the past, the new historicist still has to describe of what this 'presentness' consists. What seems to be immedi-ately surrendered in Levinson's rethinking of historicism (some-thing she did not give up so easily in the book on Wordsworth) is the present's power over the past. She repeatedly advocates a recognition of the 'present's' provisional status: the discourse she enacts only moves into configurations with others and can only be read properly – that is mis-read – in the future. To write of history is to be interpellated by it and the objective is a dialogical relation to the past which opens up spaces and does not form identities or homogenised models of knowledge. The *impossibility* of dialogue (in its humanist sense) seems to be the point:

> To return to the psychoanalytic model, criticism comes by its insights through the exaggerated and formalised alienation

of the relationship between analyst and patient – a spatial distance – and the metaphysical absurdity of its reconstructive, temporal project. To consider this absurdity an *obstacle* to the historical venture would be like viewing the analyst's distance from the analysand as a hindrance to their work. All of us who try to read the past are in similarly narrow rooms. The prison is in pretending to be uncircumstanced, in aspiring to identity.

(Levinson *et al.* 1989: 14)

This rejoicing in a negative capability is an avoidance, according to Levinson, of reification. Concluding her analysis of Wordsworth's 'new historicist' poem 'The world is too much with us' she writes 'By totalising Wordsworth's compromise solution, we make it compromise *us*. As we know from the lesson – the object lesson – of Wordsworth's poem, the other and worse option is reification.' It seems she must preserve the Romantic conception of dialogue – to rephrase Wordsworth – a person speaking to persons – thus deferring to Jerome McGann's 'humanising' tendency about which Clifford Siskin writes so interestingly (1988: 56–62). Levinson claims that history is a human product, 'essentially a form of subjectivity objectified by our temporal remove' and that the old historicism, while it could see this, failed to 'historise the subjectivity' of the present. The problem with this materialism was that it was not dialectical, that it 'failed to submit its consciousness to a critical objectification by the past' (Levinson *et al.* 1989: 28–29).

So the circumstance of the new historicist, his/her 'present-ness' is not a matter of choice. Levinson returns to this topic again and again, self-critically, almost bewildered by her own subtlety. The position of the new historicist is a question of 'historical conjunctures' she says, not 'enthusiasm' (by enthusiasm does she mean political interest?); the interest in the past is 'an *effect* of the past we study'. So what does it mean to be possessed by the past in this way, even while this past can only be constructed in the present? First, that the present as a place of enlightenment is an illusion, a hypostatic fallacy – we cannot 'know better' than that which we study, we can only misread it in interesting ways, and in so doing, note its configurative relations with other discourses and social and economic facts – that is to say, we discover what it represses and repress what it discovers. This new knowledge is not better but belated and different; it must not be transferred into an epistemology by way of an embracing theory of ideology or hegemony. This precisely is what Levinson identifies in her critical review of herself, which I take it, is the surrogate for the objectification or temporal remove from herself which she believes is necessary for the operation of the past/ present dialectic. She admits 'the inadequacy of the new historicist concept of ideology', the 'lack of a dynamic notion of ideology or a real understanding of hegemony . . . and . . . a *trans*historical notion of causality'. Thus, the past can be emptied 'of its reality, and the present of its responsibility'. This drives her back to the question of what we *should* do, but there are no answers, only a recognition that other discourses will disfigure ours, 'violate our knowledge and press out *our* Real in symbolic form' (1989: 49–51).

This request for a future generation of new historicists to locate the symbolic Real in present practice bespeaks an extraordinary paralysis, a continuing repression. To say as much is to step outside of the new historicist paradigm of course, but what seems to be happening is that analysis is required without the pain of abreaction, which here, surely, involves the rediscovery of a political unconscious. In her earlier book on Wordsworth, Levinson remarked, tellingly, 'we cannot unlearn Derrida'. In attempting to find a way through Yale's purely deconstructive paradigm, she knew that it was not to be a matter of repression. But she has surely attempted to unlearn Marx. In a lengthy footnote she describes her method by way of John Barrell's work and Fredric Jameson's, as a search for a political unconscious: by abstractive procedures the work is concretised; a subtext is located and explored to explain surface fissure or illogicality, and this leads to a reconstruction of determining conditions – the work's 'private logic' is compared to the 'social logic that overdetermines the work's presented relations' (1989: 59). This much I would understand as a method that is broadly cultural materialist. But in another footnote, she states what is left out. I summarise briefly: politics is situated around the text's allusions, probably through a 'focus on representational objects' figuring 'by displacement'. Again the models would seem to be materialist, although implicating Althusser – Jameson, Macherey. But 'politics' means actual circumstances, and these are rarely 'set within a larger and in some way compelling objective field'. We are therefore still only within the province of the performative. Although the work's figuring can denote ideological postioning, *position* is then regarded as 'a static phenomenon rather than a dynamic, problem-solving function' (Levinson *et al.* 1989: 56).

There are only representations. A post-Althusserian and probably Foucauldian scepticism about totalising ideological function means that the figurative must enjoy its status as an enclosed performance on a level of relative autonomy. What this leads to however, is the position of the present *being defined* by the object of the past that is being articulated (or more correctly, figured):

> By disengaging the Marxian content with its dramatically progressive narrative, we obstruct the development of a logic that would relate the contradiction of one age to the formations of another. Specifically, we construct for ourselves an experience of freedom and power with respect to our negotiation with the past. Of course we pay a price for this pleasure. Without the teleological framework, we cannot articulate our relation to the poetry we study, and without this articulation, our criticism must be but a weak version of that poetry: a repetition of its more vivid knowledge.
>
> (Levinson *et al.* 1989: 34)

The overbearing burden of this critical enterprise is its theoretical conscience. In protesting that we cannot stand outside of ideology, there is inevitably a complicity with its power structures. Old historicism was contiguous to Romanticism: change depends on the acquiring of knowledge, and that demands the dimension of continuity and growth. Deconstructing Romanticism however, has also led to deconstructing the same dimensions in historicism. The new historicism denies the consciousness or knowledge that is the dynamic of change.

Thus there is no position in which to situate the present, no position outside of the circle. The diametric opposite of new historicism within the frame of revised historical criticism might be that of Tony Bennett, who, in responding to the post-structuralist critique of Marxism, moves to a proposal that 'neither text nor context are conceivable as entities separable from one another' and that there can be no revival of 'objective historical meaning.' We should therefore study not texts *per se* but reading formations, the productions of meanings therefore, and the study of this *is* a process and a continuum. Moreover, it is the locus of change:

> [Texts] . . . exist only as variable pieces of play within the processes through which the struggle for their meaning is socially enacted: kept alive within the series of bids and

counter-bids which different critical tendencies advance in their attempts to organise reading practices . . . texts are thus kept alive only at the price of being always other than 'just themselves'.

For Bennett, texts are 'to be regarded as strategic sites for the contestation of dominant subject identities' – of which there are many (1987: 68). In other words, subjects are not interpellated by texts, but conduct an active interest in them, and that interest – in the broadest sense – is political.

In so many ways a brief look into new historicist practice such as this brings us back to the old disputes, disputes that are currently being conducted between cultural materialists and post-modernists. There is surely more than a whiff of post-modernism in recent new historicist writing: Lyotard's excelling in the invention of allusions, in the impossibility of presentation, is quoted by Levinson too gratefully I think, and the new historicist choreographing of deft movements which in some way emulate models discerned in the primary texts is a subtle pastiche, a celebratory entrapment within the old formations. Despite this, the new problematisation of history and context has caused a necessary crisis in our assumptions about how texts are representational of history. Equally, the endless (or potentially endless) sedimentation of historical facts serving as disinterested context is called into question. This is not to say that the past never happened, but that history never did.

References

Bennett, T. (1983). 'Texts, Readers, Reading Formations', *Literature and History*, 9:2.

—— (1987). 'Texts in History', in Geoff Bennington and Robert Young (eds.) *Post-Structuralism and the Question of History*. Cambridge, Cambridge University Press.

Butler, M. (1982). *Romantics, Rebels and Reactionaries: Romantic Literature and its Background, 1760–1830*. London and New York, Oxford University Press.

Geertz, C. (1975). *The Interpretation of Cultures*. London, Hutchinson, 1975.

Glen, H. (1983). *Vision and Disenchantment: Blake's 'Songs' and Wordsworth's 'Lyrical Ballads'*. Cambridge, Cambridge University Press.

Jameson, F. (1981). *The Political Unconscious: Narrative as a Socially Symbolic Act*. London, Methuen.

Klancher, J. (1989). 'English Romanticism and Cultural Production', in H. Aram Veeser (ed.) *The New Historicism*. London, Routledge.

LaCapra, D. (1985). *History and Criticism*. Ithaca, Cornell University Press.

Leask, N. (1988). *The Politics of Imagination in Coleridge's Critical Thought*. London, Macmillan.

Levinson, M. (1986). *Wordsworth's Great Period Poems: Four Essays*. Cambridge, Cambridge University Press.

Levinson, M., Butler, M., McGann, J., and Hamilton, P. (1986). *Rethinking Historicism*. Oxford, Blackwell.

Liu, A. (1989). 'The Power of Formalism: The New Historicism', *English Literary History*, 56:4, 721–771.

Siskin, C. (1989). *The Historicity of Romantic Discourse*. London and New York, Oxford University Press.

Smith, O. (1984). *The Politics of Romantic Language, 1791–1819*. London and New York, Oxford University Press.

White, H. (1987). *The Content of the Form: Narrative Discourse and Historical Representation*. Baltimore, Johns Hopkins University Press.

3

Hannah More's counter-revolutionary feminism

Kathryn Sutherland

What I am concerned to recover for contemporary feminist debate is a greater sense of the variety of ways in which women in periods of national crisis, like the 1790s, will treaty with or attempt to exploit the inevitable re-negotiation of the apparently fixed public/private, male/female division which underpins the political and economic model of society. In other words, how do women (conventionally ignored by history) manage their temporary introduction into history at these times? It is a question which troubled Virginia Woolf whose writing is framed by public events in the form of two world wars. Interestingly, her war-conditioned outlook makes her deeply sceptical when it comes to interpreting those minor concessions by society to women at such times as signs of any real and permanent change in its structures. Among the political advances Woolf questions are voting rights for women: she seriously doubts whether British women should use votes previously refused to them on their own terms but gained by supporting a male cause – war. (1977: 18; 168n.12) Woolf's reasoning may seem perverse; but the point to be made here, and my emphasis throughout, is what I see as late twentieth-century feminism's naive censorship of the range of women's legitimate responses in history to situations of male oppression.

I

Because women have been, and indeed largely remain, 'hidden from history' – to borrow the much-invoked phrase of the

Hazel Hare

socialist historian Sheila Rowbotham (1973) – one persistent compensatory strain in feminist literary criticism over the last twenty years (the Anglo-American empirical no less than the French theoretic variety) has emphasised the timeless availability to one another of women's shared experience. To be hidden from history, this argument implies, is to be unconstrained by, to be *freely* absent from history. Accordingly, the social modes of being which impinge on and even constitute our so-called centres of self are rendered secondary or irrelevant sources of knowledge about *women* by comparison with the indisputable counter-authority of *woman's* experience. This flight from the negative scope of history – what all women lack – to the redemptive ground of essential reality – what all women share – lays heavy stress on the totalising truth of *the* (any) woman writer's representation of (all) women, and on the inevitable authenticity of *the* (any) woman reader's response.

In positing the unchanging accessibility of women's writings to women, argument in fact contradictorily encodes as ideal and changeless the real material particularity and vulnerability to history of those all-pervasive ideological structures by which patriarchy (falsely) represents us all. The mistake has been to assume that modern consciousness is a constant of human experience. One inevitable consequence of this a-historicism has been to restrict women's literary heritage to a mutually endorsing, predictable handful of authors, almost exclusively from the late nineteenth and twentieth centuries.

A second persistent strain has been the virtually antithetical acceptance that women do live in history, and that we necessarily occupy the same political space as men: women's battles are *merely* sexual. Hence the alarming ease with which they are subsumed and reclassified within the harsher material conflicts of our historically more adept male colleagues. In this case, a simplifying politicised reading hears only the opposed dis-courses of parties and not the shared ground of women's complaints. Heard through the male-aligned rhetoric of sectarian politics, of 'left' and 'right', women writers, like women activists, are easily stripped of their fragile hold on material reality. Reduced to the 'good' or 'bad' women of history, they are abstracted from the social complex which has forged their often shared responses as women and required to represent, in absolute moral terms, the struggle's extra-historical refinement. Women's representation of historical struggle beyond history is as old as Clio and as symbolically powerful as the Statue of Liberty; but what such abstractions point to is the cautionary truth that only men engage in the material processes of history, its compromised juxtapositions as opposed to its stark moral oppositions. In the words of the French Revolutionary moderate Olympe de Gouges, who published her *Rights of Woman* in 1791, 'O women, women, when will you stop being so blind? What advantages have you gained from the revolution? A more marked distrust, a more conspicuous disdain.' Women are, she declares, 'the sex which was formerly [under the old regime] contemptible but respected, and, since the revolution, has been respectable but scorned.' (de Gouges 1979: 13–14)

For recent generations of feminists, moulded by the arguments of the so-called sexual revolution of the 1960s and '70s, what this male-aligned rhetoric has meant is a distorted preference for a 'left-wing' reading of women's history, often constructed in the teeth of the evidence. Marxist history and social histories of labour relations, in particular, have appeared to offer a women-sensitive perspective on history, because a perspective alert to the politics of oppression. But too often this has proved more effective as a strategy for displacing the story of female experience by a narrative of the emergence of class consciousness or the struggles of working men. Dorothy Thompson has written of the Chartist silencing of women's political demands in the 1840s, for example (1984: 122ff.). The possibility that the revolutionary left might prove inadequate to realising a sexually equal model for society is a doubt which some of the most historically minded women have managed to keep at bay. Conversely, women's perennial prominence in counter-revolutionary movements of the right is an uncomfortable recurrence which is rarely recognised beyond the general level.

Consequently, literary opinion still has it that Mary Wollstonecraft, writing as a radical in the 1790s, provides a positive example for women because she aligned herself with a prorevolutionary male model. Her *Vindication of the Rights of Woman* (1792) extends the leftist polemic of her own *Vindication of the Rights of Men* (1790), one of the earliest attacks upon the traditionalist rhetoric of Burke's *Reflections on the Revolution in France* (1790), and of Paine's *Rights of Man* (1791–2), to include the natural rights of women as well as men. Hannah More, however, the admirer of Burke and engaged in the same years as Wollstonecraft in producing conservative propaganda for a significantly feminised pamphlet war against the Painites and the French Revolutionary interest in Britain, must be a negative example for women. Further, the two women, the one liberated by the left and the other confined by the right, can have nothing in common, nor can their readers; so the argument goes.

Reappropriated in the 1970s as the 'mother' of modern feminism, Wollstonecraft continues to exude a personal glamour which has served to hide her historical representativeness and to distort the complexity and variety of the late eighteenth-century challenge to the masculine doctrine of rights. Barbara B. Schnorrenberg (1980) has argued the point, but she still gives disproportionate space in her essay to the 'radical' Wollstonecraft and uncritically assumes as opposition More's 'nonpolitical [sic] feminism'. More recently, Janet Todd (1988) has called vigorously for the historical reassessment of Wollstonecraft. After being long stigmatised as the enemy of women's rights, More, too, is being re-evaluated in the context of a more historically sensitive notion of female assertiveness. See, in particular, two excellent pioneer analyses by Mitzi Myers (1982; 1986).

For the modern feminist critic working to redraw the map of English literary history since the 1790s, when as Woolf tells us, 'the middle-class woman began to write' (1945: 66), the intimidating masculinist assumptions of her bi-partite model have forged a Great Tradition of women's writing which is obviously and falsely derived *via* the seductions of a left-feminist alliance. Hence projects, like Margaret Kirkham's (1983), to read Jane Austen as the disciple of Wollstonecraft; or more ambitiously in now classic handbooks, like Gilbert and Gubar's *The Madwoman in the Attic* (1979), and in multiplied women's studies survey courses, to assume a connecting thread of social subversion worked from Wollstonecraft to Austen to Charlotte Brontë to Gaskell to Eliot to Woolf. Even in Gilbert and Gubar's largely unhistoricised monolith of *the* nineteenth-century female imagination, women's creativity is represented as 'leftist' and rebellious, a kind of sublimated Chartism.

When the study appeared in 1979 it was rightly welcomed as an impressive female appropriation of Harold Bloom's influential thesis of literary paternity and as a strong challenge to the masculinist assumptions within the Anglo-American cultural tradition as a whole. But in trying too hard to counter-assert a women's literary tradition, Gilbert and Gubar sacrifice to linearity and repetition, and consequently to myth, what should be accorded to the particulars and the discontinuities of each woman writer's place in history. Their anxious and angry female author has become a prescriptive critical model of dauntingly biblical dimensions. As even adherents of their approach have noted (and most feminist rereadings are indebted to their method to some extent), theirs is a narrowly formalist argument which makes no attempt to integrate women's perceptions of themselves in art with the all-pervasive but variable constraints and sexual valuations implicit in society as a whole. Precisely because they accept the given of *woman's* absence from history, Gilbert and Gubar deny the differences between their chosen *women* authors, the subtle, historicised ways in which women treaty with, oppose, subvert, ironise, and even accommodate and contribute to cultural impositions. Consequently, too, they severely censor the list of women whom we might regard as truly women writers at all. More alarmingly, in establishing for women a strong and univocal history of literary subversion, they and their followers risk imposing as restrictive an orthodoxy on female behaviour as any dealt out by patriarchy. Even historically sensitive studies, like those recently outlined by Mary Poovey (1984) and Cora Kaplan (1985), assume a leftist (Marx through Foucault or Marxian psychoanalytical) monopoly on cultural data.

Ten years on, after a decade in which, in Britain at least, the mythic victories of a fictive but powerful post-feminism have prematurely eroded women's emergent political identity, it is a matter of urgency that feminist critics recover a subtler and more unstable historical dimension to their work. Feminist literary criticism and the provisional archaeology of those scholars working to redraw the map of English literary history would both benefit from the kind of rigorous re-evaluation of the categories 'gender' and 'history' which has been prompted among recent theorists of history (Scott 1988: 9–10). Under such critical scrutiny the apparent fixities of 'gender' and 'history' are seen to be shifting and culturally redefinable constructions, but engineered as permanently reciprocal and mutually enabling, in the process by which societies in different places and ages explain and legitimise their socio-political relations.

Characterised and confined by contemporary rhetoric as we are, to attempt to chart an alternative trajectory to that of the feminist left is to run a double risk – of exposing the modest limits of our own real progress as women in society, and of appearing unfashionably uncritical (even supportive) of the post-feminist ideology of today's New Right. Nevertheless, if we are looking to the 1790s for the emergence of a nineteenth-century women's literary tradition, a stronger contender for its founding mother may be the 'right-aligned' Hannah More than the 'left-aligned' Mary Wollstonecraft. Wary, like Woolf, of the value of political concessions to women, scornful of the female radical assumption of a sexual common ground, More builds upon and even exaggerates customary male/female distinctions. She inaugurates a counter-revolutionary female tradition. In working to sever the masculinist rhetoric of late eighteenth-century popular democracy from its revolutionary roots and to appropriate it, through acts of female domestic management, to the purposes of middle-class liberal reform, More provides a new direction and new material for women novelists like Brontë, Gaskell, and Eliot, all of whom may more appropriately be read as containing and dissipating subversion than as fuelling it.

In her introduction to the re-issued *Jane Austen and the War of Ideas*, Marilyn Butler argues that if she were beginning the book again she 'would give more consideration and a longer perspective to the conservative tradition in eighteenth-century women's writing . . . Tory feminism, I now see, is a phenomenon far too significant and enduring in the eighteenth and nineteenth centuries to be treated as merely reacting to the French Revolution with a defence of family and home – though it did that too.' (1975: p. xxxiii) Hannah More would be a good place to start. Behind her stretches a tradition of feminism reaching back to Mary Astell and drawing its strength from two sources resistant to an openly leftist or covert radical and subversive reading of women's texts – from the established Church and the discourse of Christianity; and from a firm adherence to the status quo, through which, it is clearly suggested, the privileges of rank may compensate for the weaknesses of gender. Until we come to recognise this powerful and persistent strain of feminism, we shall continue to restrict our canon of women writers and to underestimate women's social effectiveness.

There are several strong arguments for reviving Hannah More. Not least among them is the fact that she exudes none of the dangerous glamour of the 1970s reconstructions of Wollstonecraft, the sexual libertarian and would-be free woman. The ready accommodation within idealising feminist myth of the supra-historicised tragedy of Mary Wollstonecraft, the modern type of the gifted female over-reacher, *the* image of female desire, has until recently been an obstacle to the adequate contextualisation of her writings. What has always stood in the way has been a too-ready substitution of her body for her philosophies. This derives in part from the masculinist assumption that, writing from the unconscious (where else can women write from?) women must reveal their actual selves in their texts. It owes something, too, to the radical equation, early and late, of political and sexual liberties, which is never as advantageous or liberating a conjunction for women as for men; and William Godwin must take his share of the blame. His *Memoirs of the Author of a Vindication of the Rights of Woman* of 1798 exposed to public view the body of Wollstonecraft and played a significant part in the diminished assessment of her social criticism as mere autobiographical revelation.

It would be difficult to imagine, as an ideological figure, anyone less seductive than the conservative and militant Christian Hannah More. For this very reason, her feminised discourse may be a means to direct late twentieth-century feminist polemicists more effectively towards the limitations which we have too readily conspired to place on our own socio-political inquiries. Further, the obstacles which we encounter in sympathetically reconstructing More's perspectives, where no such problems exist with Wollstonecraft (so closely has she been identified with our favourite self-image), argue powerfully for the instability of the categories of 'gender' and 'history' as authoritative arrangements of knowledge and experience. As Denise Riley has recently argued, 'women' as a category does not exist in fixed relation to society. On the contrary, '"women" is a volatile collectivity in which female persons can be very differently positioned, so that the apparent continuity of the subject of "women" isn't to be relied on; "women" is both synchronically and diachronically erratic as a collectivity, while for the individual, "being a woman" is also inconstant, and can't provide an ontological foundation.' (Riley 1988: 2)

As the perpetual legitimators of political, economic, and historical men, it follows that women are fashioned according to shifting systems of representation. In the light of this insight, the realignment of 'left-wing' Wollstonecraft and 'right-wing' More allows us to constitute women's history as a more complex and more internally divided, and perhaps therefore historically more resilient, legitimation of women's negotiations with experience than has so far been allowed. What is conveniently labelled as 'women's experience' or 'the female character' is no more nor less than a politically useful shorthand, a symbolic language in which different societies located historically might articulate cultural dilemmas. Viewed in this way, More's own essentialism is itself a contingent strategy in the pursuit of female power through a theory of complementary spheres. Conversely, in recovering what Wollstonecraft and More do have in common, we also discover more forcibly just whose reality has mattered most when it comes to making history. Consequently, as women, we provide ourselves with a more powerful lever on history as event, as cultural narrative, and as institution.

II

Dorinda Outram has shown how the radical discourse of the Revolution in France was itself committed to an anti-feminine rhetoric, and she offers the challenge: 'All recent writing on women and the Revolution, which seems to emphasise women's *power*, however temporary, must explain why contemporary perceptions were so radically different.' (Outram 1987: 126) If anything, what emerges from middle-class English political writings of the late eighteenth and early nineteenth centuries is the radical male public betrayal of women, and the sense that, in their turn, women of all political persuasions were engaged in fashioning from the rhetoric of popular democracy a discourse appropriate to their peculiar needs as women. This is not a point of biology but of history; and we should not be surprised that, in the course of history, the revolutionary appropriation of the family unit which equally engaged Wollstonecraft and More in their struggle to enlarge women's sphere of activity and influence should have been transformed so surely and so ironically into the imprisoning ideology of Victorian middle-class domesticity. In literature by women we discover what women can historically articulate, and in this lies the possibility for comparison (what meanings we as critics in the present can discover in the past) and liberation (with the realisation that meaning is also open to future construction, in the sense that new significances will be duly attributed in the course of historical process).

There are two not incompatible ways of interpreting the propaganda war which More conducted with such huge success throughout the 1790s. More's might be heard as the reactive voice of conservatism working to quell pro-French sympathies in the masses and to replace a diet of political subversion with a more frugal and, to the government, a more wholesome fare. But equally, and more effectively than Wollstonecraft's purloined masculine enlightenment prose, More provides a whole battery of women-directed discourses, proposing a practical politics of domestic reformation, which is national in the ambitious scope of its campaign and personal in its focus on the woman in her family as the source of this larger regeneration.

A literary extension of her own and her sisters' charity work among the rural poor of Somerset, More's Cheap Repository series published 114 assorted monthly tracts between March 1795 and November 1797, aimed at the newly emergent middle- and lower-class readerships. For three and a half years More waged war against those radical Painite pamphleteers who, in her words, had brought 'speculative infidelity . . . down to the pockets and capacities of the poor.' (Roberts 1834: 2.458) A mixture each month of prose fictions, ballads, and adapted Bible stories, the tracts were formatted, down to eye-catching title and crude wood-cut illustration, in close imitation of the seditious pamphlets and coarse chapbooks – the traditional literature of the people – which they were intended to oust. To a large extent they were a family enterprise, written by Hannah, her sisters, and friends. 49 of them at least, those signed with the initial 'Z', are traceable to Hannah; the 'S' tracts were from her sister Sarah's (Sally's) pen (Thompson 1838: 151). The titles speak for themselves: *The Market Woman, a true tale; or Honesty is the Best Policy*; *The Riot; or Half a Loaf is better than No Bread*, a pamphlet which is popularly credited with quelling a food riot in Bristol during the grain scarcity of 1795; *The Roguish Miller; or Nothing Got by Cheating*; and *John the Shopkeeper turned Sailor; or the Folly of Going out of our Element*. The tracts retailed at the initially subsidised prices of a halfpenny or a penny; in their first year of issue alone distribution totalled two millions (Roberts 1834: 3.61). Like the high circulation figures for the cheap edition of Paine's *Rights of Man*, such staggering sales do not of course provide evidence for actual numbers of readers: middle-class radicals and conservatives alike distributed material free in job lots among the lower ranks.

Several of More's pieces were small-scale experiments in serial narration, developed episodically from one tract to the next and deploying a familiar cast of fictitious villagers whom the reader might recognise as old friends and who, in their turn, often acknowledge extra-textual affiliations with the author herself. The propagandist aim was clearly to saturate the new markets and to control their readerly perspectives. In tale after tale, literacy itself proves the key to moral conversion and economic renewal. One of the indirect objects of More's educational programme for poor children was the infiltration of their parents' reading, as several of her tracts attest (Roberts 1834: 2.459).

In the Repository Tracts as elsewhere, More targets particular social groups, distinguishing unquestioningly between 'women of rank and fortune', 'persons of the middle ranks', and 'the common people'. She deserves the familiar rebuke that her writings do nothing to unsettle the stratified model of society. But within such broad divisions she feels free to shift and redetermine her emphasis. The tracts proved so popular with the middle classes and gentry that after the first year More began to issue two versions, the second on superior paper (Roberts 1834: 2.457–8; Spinney 1939–40: 303). In Cadell's 1818 collected edition of her works, where the authorship of the 'Z' tracts is disclosed, stories originally presented 'to the inferior classes' are enlarged for the instruction of 'the middle ranks'. Recategorisation is possible because individual texts encourage women to identify themselves as a sexual solidarity across the fixed boundaries of rank or class. The village situations from which the Cheap Repository series evolved often presuppose (like many novels by women in the period) active and mixed interdependent communities of women from which the men are conveniently absent.

In other ways More's tales work to collectivise women readers through direct address or through the familiar character types of popular literature and according to their shared social and sexual vulnerabilities: as the victims of consumer pressures; as society leaders and responsible mothers; as reduced but philanthropic widows; as thrifty housewives; as the working partners of drunken labourers; as female miners; as pure village girls; and as reformed sinners. Her female portraits grow from an awareness of the exigencies of material reality for women of all ranks. The tractarian nature of More's writings makes for her contemporary women readers patterns of Christian conduct of the older types of female heroism, and also gives an indication of women's primary role in community reform in the late eighteenth century. In this way she seeks to feminise what in the rhetoric of the

Painites threatened a narrow masculinisation of the popular chapbook models derived from folklore and Bunyan.

With revisionary zeal, More takes the language of radical male agitation and tunes it to a womanly register. In place of the general public redirection demanded by the radical pamphleteers, she sets a limited and particularised social reform based on caring, enduring, and the redemptive power of women's actions. If the modern feminist reader is disquieted to detect in this an assumed political subordination of the womanly perspective, it is important to note that the active bias of More's agenda renders the family the originary site of historic endeavour. Self-evidently, periods of national crisis, like the 1790s, force the re-examination of accepted values. Within its world of intensified and exaggerated ideal divisions, gender distinctions are both reformulated and reinforced. Specifically, war brings into the public arena those values which are traditionally defined as 'private' and 'feminine'. The home, women's conventional sphere of operation, becomes the source from which are generated politically legitimating concepts like 'the national family' and 'love of country'.

This is particularly the case in those linked tales in which More herself is textually represented by the female philanthropist Mrs Jones. Introduced in the Repository Tract *The Cottage Cook; or Mrs Jones's Cheap Dishes; shewing the way to do much good with little money* (January 1797),[1] Mrs Jones is a 'great merchant's' widow in straitened circumstances and a moral revolutionary whose mission is reading itself. It is her habit 'never to walk out without a few little good books in her pocket to give away.' In her battles with swindling tradesmen, exploitative farmers, and an incompetent male hierarchy, Mrs Jones employs a system of household management which is public and political in its reverberations. An inquiry into the weight of a loaf of bread, for example, becomes the occasion for the successful exposure of a dishonest baker and for a lecture on the necessity of sometimes turning informer, for the good of society as a whole.

More particularly, Mrs Jones is a champion of the rights of women – their rights to a useful, practical education and to a sober, home-centred husband. If, as the contemporary complaint was, Tom Paine took labouring men out of the home and into the alehouse to debate the 'rights of man', Mrs Jones campaigns on behalf of women and children against the divisiveness and misery of drink. '[W]hile the man is enjoying himself, as it is called, his wife and children are ragged and starving', she grimly declares. The threat posed by alcohol and public houses to lower-class stability was the focus of reformist endeavour from the late eighteenth century. The ruinous consequences of excessive drinking are illustrated in several of More's own tracts: *The Carpenter; or the Danger of Evil Company* (March 1795); *The Gin Shop; or a Peep into a Prison* (March 1795); *The History of Hester Wilmot* (June–July 1797).

In *The History of Mr Fantom, the New-Fashioned Philosopher, and his Man William* (August 1797), William refuses to work but 'got drunk, or read the *Rights of Man*'. (More 1818: 4. 33) The comment forms part of the late revision and expansion of the tale for *Stories for the Middle Ranks*. As issued in 1818, during the dangerous reawakening of radical unrest, the insult is as relevant a piece of conservative propaganda as it would have been in 1797. In the tract as originally published, More has her female representative of good sense, Mrs Fantom, observe of William to her husband, 'the new-fashioned philosopher': 'He was at first very orderly and obedient, but now he is seldom sober of an evening, and in the morning, when he should be rubbing the tables in the parlour, he is generally lolling upon them and reading your little manual of the new philosophy.' It should come as no surprise that William is hanged for theft at the close of the tale.

Mrs Jones literally revolutionises the obscure village of Weston to which she has retired on her husband's bankruptcy and death. Here she exploits the ineffectual and largely careless male hierarchy of Sir John, the Squire, the Parson, the Attorney, and the Doctor in the practical execution of her plans; and she conspires with the village women for the improvement of their condition. Between them the women have Mr Crib the baker brought to court and fined; Mr Wills the shopkeeper is forced to bring his trading practices in line with those of Mrs Sparks, the female grocer; of the three village pubs, they drive two out of business; and by various small initiatives, they contrive in the scope of the tract's sixteen pages to transfer the management and profit of the village economy into women's hands. The narrator explains the practical justice of this:

Mrs Jones was much respected by all the rich persons in Weston, who had known her in her prosperity. Sir John was thoughtless, lavish and indolent. The Squire was over-frugal but active, sober, and not ill-natured. Sir John loved pleasure, the Squire loved money. Sir John was one of those popular sort of people who get much praise and yet do little good . . . so she shewed her good sense by never asking Sir John for advice, or the Squire for subscriptions, and by this prudence gained the full support of both.

. . .

Patty Smart and Jenny Rose were thought to be the two best managers in the parish . . . Mrs Jones found . . . that Patty and Jenny contrived to brew as well as to bake. She sent for these women, knowing that from them she could get truth and reason.

Mrs Jones's exertions here and in the subsequent linked tales *The Sunday School* and *The History of Hester Wilmot* (in two parts) (May–July 1797), where she founds a Sunday school and continues to train the village women in domestic management, are closely based on the activities of Hannah and her younger sister Martha (Patty) among the Mendip villagers. The slatternly village economy of the unregenerate Weston is that of Cheddar, which, fictionalised, becomes the type of every English community in need of female regulation and wise management. In Cheddar the Mores were shocked at the affluence, brutality, and obstructiveness of the local farmers ('these rich savages'), the negligence and ineffectuality of the clergy, and the desperate poverty and ignorance of the labourers. Martha confided to her journal: 'there is as much knowledge of Christ in the interior of Africa as there is to be met with in this wretched, miserable place.' (Roberts 1859: 16) The comparison was not extravagant. Among the glass workers of Nailsea and the miners of Shipham and Rowberrow the sisters were exposed to considerable danger: 'the people savage, and depraved almost even beyond Cheddar, brutal in their natures, and ferocious in their manners. They began by suspecting we should make our fortunes by selling their children as slaves. No constable would venture to arrest a Shipham man, lest he should be concealed in one of their pits, and never be heard of more; no uncommon case.' (Roberts 1859: 28) Martha's account of a visit to a Mendip glass factory in 1792, with its humorous documentation of male timidity and female enterprise, establishes the origin of Mrs Jones's feminine militancy, her dismissal of male authority, and the shrewd appeal to lower-class self-interest in her Christian message:

Whatever we had seen before was of a different nature, and, though we had encountered savages, hard-hearted farmers, little cold country gentry, a supercilious and ignorant corporation, yet this was still new, and unlike all other things . . . Both sexes and all ages herding together; voluptuous beyond belief. The work of a glass-house is an irregular thing, uncertain whether by day or by night; not only infringing upon man's rest, but constantly intruding upon the privileges of the Sabbath. The wages high, the eating and drinking luxurious – the body scarcely covered, but fed with dainties of a shameful description. The high buildings of the glass-houses ranged before the doors of these cottages – the great furnaces roaring – the swearing, eating, and drinking of these half-dressed, black-looking beings, gave it a most infernal and horrible appearance. . . . We had a gentleman with us who, being rather personally fearful, left us to pursue our own devices, which we did by entering and haranguing every separate family. We were in our usual luck respecting personal civility, which we received even from the worst of these creatures, some welcoming us to 'Botany Bay', others to 'Little Hell', as they themselves shockingly called it. We talked to them a great deal, and indeed they all listened, and some with great, and I may add with truth, delightful attention. We were too prudent in this first visit to drop a word that did not imply something creditable – making good servants, getting top places, going out into the world, &c. Religion here would have been a very indiscreet, and, I fear, unsuccessful beginning.

(Roberts 1859: 61–2)

Urged on by the Evangelical reformer William Wilberforce, who matched their exertions with generous financial aid, the sisters began their mission of enlightenment auspiciously enough in the Revolutionary autumn of 1789. Their education programme – Sunday schools and, in some parishes, weekday 'Schools of Industry', and later Sunday evening classes for parents and young men and women – started with 140 children. By the end of 1791, Martha could write that they 'have now taken in hand ten parishes, and have the care of near one thousand children.' (Roberts 1859: 48) In Cheddar the pioneering enterprise was exclusively female and a carefully executed colonisation of male space. In only a month Hannah and Martha opened a Sunday school and a weekday school with three mistresses, where thirty girls might learn to read, sew, knit, and spin. Their teachers, 'these excellent women', also included in their duties medical, financial, and spiritual assistance for the sick, and 'in all respects did just what a good clergyman does in other parishes.' (Roberts 1859: 51–2) Such services laid the foundation for the Women's Clubs and Friendly Societies which the Mores established from August 1792. (Roberts 1859: 63ff.; Roberts 1834: 2.304–5)

To read Martha's *Mendip Annals* and Hannah's correspondence of the early 1790s alongside the subsequent Cheap Repository Tracts is to be made aware of the ready adaptation of edifying fact to exemplary fiction. Hannah's real-life 'excellent women' provide in the details of their histories the seeds of subsequent chapbook tales. In her principal teacher, Mrs Baber, she found 'a woman of excellent natural sense, great knowledge of the human heart, activity, zeal, and uncommon piety. She had had a good fortune for one in middle life, but a wicked son had much reduced it.' (Roberts 1859: 51) Hester Wilmot, the model Sunday-school pupil of More's tracts, evinces the kind of spiritual conversion and progress which the Mendip education programme was established to encourage. From a rebellious and illiterate girl, Hester is transformed by Sunday-school attendance into a diligent and obedient worker, a domestic heroine. In the course of her history we see her hard-earned savings gambled away by a drunken father; but by prayer and good example she is the means to his reclamation. Eventually she converts both father and mother to More's brand of Evangelical Christianity, and at Mrs Jones's annual school outing and feast, it is Hester who wins the prize of 'a handsome Bible'. Her tale concludes: 'Hester continues to grow in grace and in knowledge. Last Christmas-day she was appointed an under teacher in the school; and many people think that some years hence, if any thing should happen to Mrs Crew, Hester may be promoted to be head mistress.'

In their feminisation of value, in the concerned depiction of the poor and their reformation by middle-class practices, and in the promotion of the family as the model for the non-violent reorganisation of society, More's tales are to be compared with the regional narratives of social concern of her contemporaries Maria Edgeworth and Elizabeth Hamilton. With Edgeworth, More shares the belief that education can dissolve political grievances. In The *Cottagers of Glenburnie* (1808) Hamilton's reformist narrator, the appropriately named Mrs Mason, and her educational programme are derived from More and the Cheap Repository Tracts. More herself is clearly indebted to the example of Sarah Trimmer. Trimmer's *Family Magazine; or a Repository of Religious Instruction, and Rational Amusement. Designed to counteract the pernicious tendency of immoral books, &c. which have circulated of late years among the inferior classes of people, to the obstruction of their improvement in religion and morality* (1788–9) was a weighty monthly miscellany containing improving discourses, general interest pieces, 'monthly occurences', cookery hints and recipes – like 'The Frugal Housewife' for January 1789, being 'A meal for three or four persons, which will cost only four-pence' – a regular 'Gardener's Kalendar', and several serial features. Among these are 'Village Dialogues' (from January 1789), in which Robert the ploughman and his sweetheart the maid-servant Betty discourse on a variety of topics and in the process reveal as comforting a respect for the values of an ideal social middle as will Jack Anvil in More's *Village Politics* (1793). Elsewhere, in 'Moral Tales', which centre around the village lives and philanthropic activities of Mr and Mrs Andrews, a couple in the middle rank, we find the model for More's Mrs Jones, as 'The Village Festival; or Merit Rewarded', the 'Moral Tale' for July 1788, suggests:

> It was mentioned in a former tale that Mr and Mrs Andrews had concerted a scheme with the neighbouring gentry, for promoting conjugal happiness in the village, and that preparatory to it a paper was dispersed, concerning the proper behaviour of husbands and wives. . . . In order to promote good housewifery, Mrs Andrews promised to give to every woman who had a family of children, whose cloaths, as well as her own, were kept tidily mended, a new *petticoat*, or any other article of dress she should most stand in need of. . . . In the course of the year Mrs Andrews had made it her business frequently to inspect the apparel, and question the women: and very high pleasure had she received, from finding all the houses neat, the children tidy, and every thing well mended, excepting in a few places, where sickness had prevented the women and girls from exerting themselves as they wished to do. – It is needless to say, that allowances were made for them, and relief afforded. – The others received certificates from Mrs Andrews, in which,

with great delight, she mentioned, that family peace had met
with very little interruption.

(Trimmer 1788: 461–4)

In her turn, More can be seen as inaugurating the nineteenth-
century tradition of 'realistic' female social fiction as displayed in
the work of Elizabeth Stone, Charlotte Tonna, and Geraldine
Jewsbury. Together with Charlotte Brontë's Shirley Keeldar and
Caroline Helstone, with Gaskell's Margaret Hale, and with Eliot's
Dorothea Brooke, More's own Mrs Jones shares an affinity with
children, with semi-literate labourers, with victimised women
workers, with the socially insecure and historically neglected.
The type endures, politically muted, in Woolf's Mrs Ramsay and
Mrs Dalloway. Their domestic centrality is maintained in direct
opposition to what their female creators consider the extravagant, self-regarding and ultimately peripheral heroics of progressive male thinkers.

Elsewhere, in *The History of Mr Fantom*, More mocks, among
other radical male thinkers, Thomas Paine and Wollstonecraft's
partner William Godwin with their universal schemes for human
advancement, setting them against the effectiveness of women's
more limited goals. Mr Fantom is 'the new-fashioned philosopher', who has 'a plan in [his] head for relieving the miseries of
the whole world.' But 'in his zeal to make the whole world free
and happy, [he] was too prudent to include his wife.' In spite of
this, however, and in a section which More expanded to
highlight middle-class women's influential activities for the
tract's republication among *Stories for the Middle Ranks of Society*
(1818), Mrs Fantom and her daughter carry through several
charitable plans to relieve suffering in the local community. Their
female heroics, though minutely practical, are dramatically
effective. Mrs Fantom attends to the trivialities of life with an
adventurous spirit, while her husband looks on from a philo-
sophic distance. At one point she rushes out into the night, her
pockets 'stuffed . . . with old baby linen' (More 1818: 38), to lend
assistance at the scene of a village fire. Baby linen, it turns out, is
just what is needed! Her husband, the philosopher, absents
himself. The narrator observes acidly,

. . . the present distress was neither grand enough nor far
enough from home to satisfy the wide-stretched
benevolence of the philosopher, who sat down within sight

of the flames to work at a new pamphlet, which now
swallowed up his whole soul, on universal benevolence.

(More 1818: 33)

Importantly in More's analysis, it is the very particularity of
women's assigned vision which is able to generate in times of
crisis those precise social understandings which elude the
unwieldy masculine universalising tendency. In its specificity it
may be that women's historical sense, too, is a subtler faculty.

More's conduct books for the lower orders can legitimately be
seen as complementing her conduct books for young ladies of the
middle and upper ranks: most particularly *Strictures on the Modern
System of Female Education* (1799), where she writes:

> Young ladies should also be accustomed to set apart a fixed
> portion of their time as sacred to the poor, whether in
> relieving, instructing, or working for them; and the perform-
> ance of this duty must not be left to the event of contingent
> circumstances, or the operation of accidental impressions;
> but it must be established into a principle, and wrought into
> a habit. A specific portion of time must be allotted to it, on
> which no common engagement must be allowed to intrench.
>
> (More 1799: 1.117–18)

Where in these longer works the portrait of More's ideal woman
served to contest society's dominant definitions of sexuality and
female desirability, in the Repository Tracts the newly constructed woman proves her social and political worth by confronting and conquering the harmful divisiveness which lower-
class culture threatens in the state. More's argument, and the
principle on which her heroines act, is that in changing the
household we influence history. More and her female agents
sense the contingency of the political and the domestic. We in our
turn, and as sensitive post-Foucauldian readers, see in the
dynamics of their narratives how the renegotiated terms of
female sexuality might function as the signs of wider cultural
changes, notably in class relations, with one corporate fiction (the
reformist female) engendering another (the tractable and indus-
trious workforce).

In *Betty Brown, the St Giles's Orange Girl; with some account of Mrs
Sponge the Money-Lender* (August 1796), Betty's spiritual and
economic prosperity stems from her denial of her old lawless
associates and her betrayal of her corrupt landlady Mrs Sponge.
Betty's true benefactress, 'the lady', is the wife of 'one of the

Justices of the new Police' and is herself a moral policewoman of formidable energy. She sets the poor orange seller on the path to redemption (*via* the local Sunday school) and teaches her those 'Rules for Retail Dealers' which will ensure her the degree of upward mobility agreeable to her station. The whole narrative works to expose the mutual exploitation of those at the bottom of society and to enforce the beneficial workings of vertical relations while denying the value of lateral ties.

The two-stage reformulation of the female which More outlines becomes a major preoccupation of the nineteenth-century industrial novel. In the narratives of Gaskell and Eliot, for example, a familiar pattern is established whereby the middle-class heroine firstly renegotiates the terms which constitute ideal femininity, enlarging them to include intellectual, active, and especially philanthropic characteristics; secondly, she tests these qualities in situations of class conflict, where she redeems subversive elements or quietens political unrest through a tactical programme of education and 'socialisation'. Like More's tracts, the industrial novel often promotes the activities of this new woman – in particular, her ability both to align herself with and to depoliticise lower-class unrest – in contradistinction to an older established male order. Cutting through a bankrupt patriarchal model of social relations, the new woman elevates the practices of a contrasting female domain. The inference is clear – that the unreformed past belonged to the men but the forward-thinking individual, the type of the modern social consciousness, is woman.

Betty Brown's 'lady', like the army of philanthropic middle-class women who march through Victorian life and fiction, represents the new dispensation:

> 'You shall attend a Sunday School, where you will be taught these good things, and I will promote you as you shall be found to deserve.'
>   Poor Betty here burst into tears of joy and gratitude, crying out, 'What! shall such a poor friendless creature as I be treated so kindly and learn to read the word of God too? O, Madam, what a lucky chance brought me to your door.' – 'Betty,' said the lady, 'what you have just said, shews the need you have of being better taught; there is no such thing as chance, and we offend God when we call that luck or chance which is brought about by his will and pleasure.

> None of the events of your life have happened by chance –
> but all have been under the direction of a good and kind
> Providence. . . . Above all, you must bless his goodness in
> sending you to me, not only because I have been of use to
> you in your worldly affairs, but because he has enabled me to
> shew you the danger of your state from sin and ignorance,
> and to put you in a way to know his will and to keep his
> commandments.'

But it is the lady, not her husband the magistrate and certainly
not God, who sets out the commandments (those 'Rules for Retail
Dealers') by which the new Betty should live; and it is Hannah
More's providential authority which promises to reward her
conversion with a sequel, telling how 'Betty, by industry and
piety, rose in the world, till at length she came to keep a
handsome sausage-shop near the seven-dials, and was married
to an honest Hackney coachman.'

III

Since the 1790s commentators have been quick to point out that
'right-wing' More and 'left-wing' Wollstonecraft can sound
surprisingly similar in certain of their arguments (Myers
1982: 203). What they have been slow to detect is the feminist
power which accrues to More's articulation of their differences.
For all its extension to the sexual sphere of the revolutionary
rationalist doctrine of rights, *A Vindication of the Rights of Woman* is
forced into bargaining for concessions similar to those which
More's counter-revolutionary propaganda proposes for the
strengthening of domestic security in the face of international
crisis. Unlike More, Wollstonecraft theorises professions for
middle-class women at least, who in consequence might become
physicians or businesswomen or even study politics (1975: 260–
2). But very like More, because sexually confined within the same
commercial and proto-industrial environment, Wollstonecraft
cannot imagine a woman's life as at any level a self-productive
unit. As there is in any minimally advanced society no economy
of one; so women are particularly called upon to reproduce the
mutuality and interdependence of the commercial model in the
concept of the family. What is economically confining is psycho-
logically compelling. Neither writer, ultimately, can imagine
women as occupying any other than the nurturing role: this is
women's work. Women should be educated, not in order to

participate in public life, but chiefly that they may become more rational wives and mothers. This is as insistently the argument of the *Vindication* as its obverse is the complaint of Wollstonecraft's fiction – that mothers, and *not* fathers, have established an inheritance of female passivity and suffering, confined by which one generation of women will continue to repudiate and betray the next. Significantly, the greatest liberation which either Wollstonecraft or More conceives is a socially productive widow-hood, surrounded by dependents, but released for the future from the constraints of sexual attractiveness and reproduction.

Like More, Wollstonecraft would extend women's sphere of influence by extending their affective lives beyond the transient youthful goals of sexual pleasure and marriage, to include friendship, rational companionship between the sexes, and responsible motherhood. Both insist that to widen the foundation of women's education is to raise their capacity for virtuous citizenship, but that, in Wollstonecraft's words, 'everything conspires to render the cultivation of the understanding more difficult in the female than the male world.' (1975: 144) This is so, argues More in *Strictures on . . . Female Education*, because a 'consummate knowledge of the world' is not open to 'a delicate woman', 'which could she attain, she would never be supposed to have come honestly by.' (1799: 2.24–5) In Chapter 3 of the *Vindication* Wollstonecraft makes a plea for revolution which is implicitly domestic and is sustained by her sense of breakdown in the sexual economy of the family: 'It is time to effect a revolution in female manners – time to restore to them their lost dignity – and make them, as a part of the human species, labour by reforming themselves to reform the world.' (1975: 132) The passage which follows rounds off her critique of Rousseau's description of necessary female subordination, by which, she claims, he gives 'a sex to mind' (p. 128). Women are, in Rousseau's comprehension, by nature unfit for higher contemplation, and their rational capacity is but the sign of their obedient pupilage to the males, their natural tutors. Deprived of a husband's knowing restraint, women will sink, more deeply enthralled to that delicate sensibility and accommodation to pleasure by which they collaborate in their own oppression. Against Rousseau, Wollstonecraft comes close to arguing that sensibility operates as female false consciousness whose power will dissolve before a reformed education programme which admits women's rational equality with men.

Protesting vigorously against the exclusion of women from social dignity by male intellectuals of all persuasions, Wollstonecraft counters with her own ideal career for a woman. Challenging Rousseau's emphasis on women's accommodation to sensual pleasure and their natural pupil-state, she dresses her ideal woman as a fruitful and independent mother. 'Let fancy now present a woman', she begins; and she continues, mapping her progress through marriage 'from affection' (not passion), to an early and impoverished widowhood, when, 'softened . . . into melancholy resignation, her heart turns to her children with redoubled fondness, and . . . affection gives a sacred heroic cast to her maternal duties . . . Raised to heroism by misfortunes, she . . . in the bloom of life forgets her sex. . . . Her children have her love, and her brightest hopes are beyond the grave, where her imagination often strays.' 'I think I see her', Wollstonecraft continues,

> surrounded by her children, reaping the reward of her care. The intelligent eye meets hers, whilst health and innocence smile on their chubby cheeks, and as they grow up the cares of life are lessened by their grateful attention. She lives . . . to see her children attain a strength of character sufficient to enable them to endure adversity without forgetting their mother's example.
>
> The task of life thus fulfilled, she calmly waits for the sleep of death, and rising from the grave, may say – 'Behold, Thou gavest me a talent, and here are five talents.'
>
> (pp. 138–9)

The vision is depressing and significant. Arrogating to herself the sibylline privilege of shaping the future in words, and temporarily freed by fancy from the laws of necessity, Wollstonecraft aspires no higher than a compromised and severe accommodation to the socio-economic strictures of her present. Acknowledging the material grounds of women's inequality, the vision not only extinguishes her plea for a more even distribution of resources, but demonstrates that, short-changed though she is in her dealings with society, woman, 'without a sufficient provision', will nevertheless return five talents for one. Forgoing women's rights to material equality in favour of her labour for, and recompense from, a higher, spiritual tribunal, Wollstonecraft's vignette effectively renders women's rights post-historical and, familiar exchange, trades material welfare for moral rewards.

Wollstonecraft's source, the parable of the talents, from Matthew 25, is also firmly in place behind More's productive widow Mrs Jones. But in her case the exemplar has lost none of its original economic force and, consequently, none of its feminist potential. On the contrary, the unquestioning confidence with which More draws on the universalistic language of Christianity appears to free her from those contradictions and self-divisions which distort rationalist discourse on Wollstonecraft's lips. In particular, Christian rhetoric dissolves for More what is a serious obstacle for Wollstonecraft – that is the moral vulnerability of the concept of experience as applied to women and the potential instability which it can uncover in women's identities as natural and social beings. Wollstonecraft's partially appropriated rationalism is founded on the misogynist assumption that restrained as the objects of male regard women are socially serviceable, but as self-regarding subjects, they are dangerous. The trap is a sensitive one and room for manoeuvre is tight: if lack of experience has traditionally rendered women too innocent for full participation in society, then, equally, the well-attested corrupting properties of experience when gained provide them with a firm disincentive to act on their own behalf.

Curiously, as the ultimate test of female worth, inexperience – purity – is a more imprisoning concept within rationalist than within Christian discourse. One reason for this is undoubtedly that the simple sexual presuppositions of Christianity are more or less impervious to social reconstruction and consequently, once acknowledged, more easily set aside. Beyond this, Christian rhetoric clearly provides the authority to subsume feminine weakness within Christian usefulness; and more importantly a code which encourages the surmounting of sexual difference itself. The Christian is Christian first and gendered second. As More points out in *Strictures on . . . Female Education*, in Christ 'there is neither "male nor female".' (1799: 2.30) Not only this, but through the example of Christ himself, the language and ideology of Christianity represent the legitimation of so-called feminine values, and, as More is quick to argue, the superiority of the female sex: 'And as the final hope of the female sex is equal, so are their present means, perhaps, more favourable, and their opportunities, often, less obstructed than those of the other sex.

In their Christian course women have every superior advantage . . .' (2.31). More continues:

> I would call on women to reflect that our religion has not only
> made them heirs to a blessed immortality hereafter, but has
> greatly raised them in the scale of being here, by lifting them
> to an importance in society unknown to the most polished
> ages of antiquity. The religion of Christ has even bestowed a
> degree of renown on the sex beyond any other religion.
>
> (2.39)

More's argument is, of course, a justification of the separate
spheres of the two sexes (women's superiority in part consisting
in the dubious 'privilege' of their exclusion from classical and
pagan learning [2.32–4]); as such it certainly contributes to the
soothing middle-class notion of a contained female domestic
subculture. But it is much more than this. In fact, More borrows
the authority of her Christian discourse to validate women's
renegotiation of certain gender assumptions within her own
society; specifically, assumptions about women's role in the
national economy. Critics have begun to reassess More's influence on the middle-class redirection of British society in the late
eighteenth century (though it is her literary and Evangelical
importance rather than her effect, if any, on political reform
which is under review). But what they have not attended to is
how far for her the middle route, between rulers and ruled,
implied something like gender liberation.

For Wollstonecraft, women 'in the middle class . . . appear to
be in the most natural state.' (1975: 81) For More, activated by a
similar autobiographical compulsion, the middle ground is
equally sexually empowering. In neither case is this surprising:
during the eighteenth century the terms of cultural discourse
marked out the notional middle increasingly as a feminine and
feminised space. Obviously, and in the long term, what was
effected was not a feminisation of social models but a masculine
consolidation of this so-called feminine middle ground. But in the
late eighteenth and early nineteenth centuries, when the divisions and alignments of the new proto-industrial society were
still dangerously unstable, it was possible for women to play
active roles in legitimising the middle class as *the* hegemonic
group. The daughter of a humble schoolmaster and a woman
who, even in her early 'secular' career, had infiltrated many male

centres of influence (notably the Garrick circle), More herself played a key part in criticising aristocratic mores. Her Church context – the Clapham sect – was professional rather than aristocratic, and in the course of her reformist writing programme she moved from the inculcation of middle-class values in the lowest classes to their promotion among the aristocracy. She was in this sense a progressive rather than a traditionalist, and her Evangelical vision of wholesale social reform from palace to cottage was certainly as revolutionary as, and more influential than, Wollstonecraft's agenda. According to Gerald Newman, in an article which sets More's work in its wider context, it is important when dealing with the Clapham sect to make the significant distinction between political loyalty and cultural subversion. Though 'loyalist', 'neo-puritans' like More and Wilberforce and their middle-class supporters 'did much more indeed to subvert the established order than to uphold it. Abstractly evident in all their projects . . . was a determined effort to strike down many of the fundamental traditions of the country.' (Newman 1975: 401) Hence Newman's conclusion that they should be regarded 'as moral and social revolutionaries'.

More's understanding of the middle is ideologically more firmly rooted, more prescient than Wollstonecraft's. From the colonising model of the social middle comes the late eighteenth-century politicisation of the family as the site of social identity in history and the generative model for larger political and economic relations. Central to this model, in Adam Smith's influential explanation, is the limited, practical perspective of the female. In Book 5 of *The Wealth of Nations* (1776), Smith extols the usefulness of women's education and the equation which can be drawn between the labour required to achieve it and the profit it brings; no part of the effort expended is wasted:

> There are no publick institutions for the education of women, and there is accordingly nothing useless, absurd, or fantastical in the common course of their education. . . . Every part of their education tends evidently to some useful purpose; either to improve the natural attractions of their person, or to form their mind to reserve, to modesty, to chastity, and to œconomy: to render them both likely to become the mistresses of a family, and to behave properly when they have become such. In every part of her life a woman feels some conveniency or advantage from every

part of her education. It seldom happens that a man, in any part of his life, derives any conveniency or advantage from some of the most laborious and troublesome parts of his education.

(Smith 1976a: 2.781)

Clearly Smith was no feminist; but there is a feminist opportunity in the congruence of certain elements within his commercial perspective with More's female-friendly Evangelical model.

In the writings of the eighteenth-century political economists, much consideration was given to the problem of how the commercial society might preserve its institutional stability and the 'virtue' of its people while at the same time stimulating wants and extending prosperity (as the success of the commercial model dictated that it should) even down to its lowest ranks. In the process of debate, the understanding of virtue as a suitable attribute of the individual in the political community was necessarily reformulated. It has been thoroughly argued that one derivation of virtue in eighteenth-century thought was from the civic humanist ideal as represented to later ages by the Graeco-Roman city republics (Pocock 1975; 1983). In the terms of this old-established tradition, virtue was martial virtue, and the practice of citizenship lay with a restricted propertied élite whose duty committed them to an undelegated military activism. As a pattern it emphasised both the public and the undivided identity of the citizen. The conditions for a commercial society, however – for the kind of society which eighteenth-century Britain increasingly represented – could be seen to lead its members in a contrary direction, success depending now on the promotion of a privatised self-interest and the progressive division and delegation of civic duties. The terms of debate – the active exercise of citizenship, on the one hand, and the private satisfaction of needs on the other – afforded no easy assimilation. But among the many restatements of the nature of virtue in a commercial society, those associated with the family and with women's role in the family are worth rehearsing here.

It is obvious that, in the old definition, virtue and the concept of citizenship were exclusively aristocratic and male. In its redefinition, as a concept of manners, what is noticeable is how the conjugal family and the middle-class household come to replace the military model in forming the virtuous citizen, and how for some theorists the domestic affections and the family unit are no longer subordinate to public good but are to be seen as the original network of social obligations. The shift can be heard in the influential writings of the Scottish intellectuals, in Francis Hutcheson's early linking of military-political humanism with a new system of social morality, and in the later market-sensitive redefinition of virtue in the work of Adam Smith, his pupil at Glasgow University. For Hutcheson, whose *System of Moral Philosophy* (1755) appeared only after his death, the domestic affections were 'the highest satisfactions of life' and 'the chiefest springs of industry, and an incitement to zeal for our country's defence, and to all honourable services.' (1755: 2.187) For Smith in 1790, the family is the best training ground for a wider social commerce:

> Domestic education is the institution of nature; public education, the contrivance of man. It is surely unnecessary to say, which is likely to be the wisest. . . . Among well-disposed people, the necessity or conveniency of mutual accommodation, very frequently produces a friendship not unlike that which takes place among those who are born to live in the same family. Colleagues in office, partners in trade, call one another brothers; and frequently feel towards one another as if they really were so. Their good agreement is an advantage to all . . .
>
> (Smith 1976b: 222–4)

Gradually, in place of the vigilance and courage necessary to the preservation of the state, we find established in eighteenth-century debate those family virtues more suited to the requirements of the market – namely, prudence, discretion, and industry. These emergent middle-class characteristics will eventually become influential over the whole range of activities in society. For example, the powerful *Edinburgh Review* (founded in 1803), that later organ of Scottish cultural thinking, saw an ideally constituted middle as tempering the reading tastes of those above and below it and fashioning from its literary interpretations the determining representations of everyday life for society as a whole. For More, writing in *Strictures on . . . Female Education*, the 'common saying' should still hold true 'that most worth and virtue are to be found in the middle station.' (1799: 1.63)

What we need to recapture is the complex domestic recourse of much eighteenth-century political economic discussion. On the one hand, there is the linguistic evidence: the regulation and wise administration of the ideal economy are in some accounts described in terms still close enough to their generating matrix to suggest the earlier more restricted application to the 'œconomy' of the household (from the Greek *oikonomia*, 'the administration of the household'). Indeed, throughout the eighteenth century the unattributed term 'economy' retained as its primary significance 'the management of a house' or 'domestic regulation'. 'Political economy', cited in the OED from 1767, is, like the concept's botanical and zoological applications at this time, a metaphoric extension of the domestic context. When the word stands alone, as in Smith's usage in the extract quoted from *The Wealth of Nations*, and in More's description of Mrs Jones as a woman who has 'lately studied œconomy' for herself, household regulation is to be understood. It is not until much later that the position is reversed and *'home* economics' becomes the concessionary term.

On the other hand, there is Adam Smith himself. Legitimately or by distortion, Smith's work has been seen as a point of departure and occupies a key place in the development of modern economic discourse. His stature is such that he tends to eclipse his near-contemporary thinkers. In particular, his inquiry into the wealth of nations is transitional in its rejection of the older model of the household *œconomy* as exemplary of the national *economy*. But against that, his contemporary James Steuart was still content to establish his massive *Inquiry into the Principles of Political Œconomy* (1767) on the old basis. Steuart begins his survey with a confident analogy: 'Œconomy in general is the art of providing for all the wants of a family, with prudence and frugality . . . What œconomy is in a family, political œconomy is in a state . . .' (1767: 1.1–2) In addition, and complicatingly, Steuart's household organisation is patriarchal, with a 'lord and steward' at its head; for Smith, though he avoids the model of the 'œconomy' of the household, a feminised space is assumed as generative of long-term economic good. Not only does he consider the enclosed family group to be the nursery of some of the best characteristics of modern commercial man; but in the household's capacity for consumption is found a vital stimulus to large-scale production.

We have scarcely begun to assess the effects on women's opportunities in society and on the discourse of femininity of the attempts of interested groups throughout the eighteenth century to define and appropriate the structure of the household. In particular, we need to weigh the implications of competing economic representations of society for women's encounters with a variety of public discourses. What is empowering in More's 'œconomic' language is the extended range made available to her through the female reappropriation of this publicly appropriated space. Further, if the conservative propaganda of the war years emphasised the identity of political and moral perspectives, it also gave national authority to a feminised notion of domestic management. An adept at redeploying universalising discourses and at hijacking the language and tropes of the opposition, More makes full use of this legitimating rhetoric to insert woman at the centre of things. For example, Adam Smith's famous 'invisible hand', which directs the larger economic mechanism and promotes long-term universal benefit, (1976a: 1.456) is isolated in More's argument as a feminine principle ordering society in direct imitation of He who superintends the universe. The description occurs in *Strictures . . . on Female Education*, where More appears to concur with Smith on women's education. But note how what was reduced to the serviceable example in Smith's domestic appropriation has become, in More's reappropriation, a vision of extended female boundaries:

> The chief end to be proposed in cultivating the understandings of women, is to qualify them for the practical purposes of life . . . The great uses of study are to enable her to regulate her own mind, and to be useful to others. . . . She should pursue every kind of study which will teach her to elicit truth; which will lead her to be intent upon realities; will give precision to her ideas; will make an exact mind. . . . Every kind of knowledge which is rather fitted for home consumption than foreign exportation, is peculiarly adapted to women. . . . Œconomy, such as a woman of fortune is called on to practise, is not merely the petty detail of small daily expences . . . but it is the exercise of a sound judgment exerted in the comprehensive outline of order, of arrangement, of distribution; of regulations by which alone well governed societies, great and small, subsist. She, who has the best regulated mind will, other things being equal, have the best regulated family. As in the superintendence of the universe, wisdom is seen in its *effects*; and as in the visible works of Providence, that which goes on with such beautiful

regularity is the result not of chance but of design; so that management which seems the most easy is commonly the consequence of the best concerted plan. A sound œconomy is a sound understanding brought into action; it is calculation realised; it is the doctrine of proportion reduced to practice; it is foreseeing consequences and guarding against them; it is expecting contingencies and being prepared for them.

(1799: 2.1–6)

Among More's early friends was the economist and cleric Josiah Tucker, Dean of Gloucester and later of Bristol. Like Smith, Tucker was an advocate of progressive commercialisation and well-read in the Scottish school of Hutcheson and others. A neglected and eccentric figure, he is remembered for his dispute with David Hume over the theoretic consequences of free trade between rich and poor countries. His independent approach has been described by J.G.A. Pocock as that of 'a progressive conservative, the defender of a commercial order perhaps not much older than himself' who 'sees no contradiction . . . between upholding the Whig commercial order and maintaining the primacy of the landed interest.' (Pocock 1985: 184–5) Most importantly for the present argument, however, Tucker's views on a variety of moral and economic issues might be seen as influential upon More's practical philanthropy.

Tucker saw in commerce nothing incompatible with God's providential plan for the universe, arguing in one published sermon 'On the Connection and Mutual Relation between Christian Morality, Good Government, and National Commerce'. Tucker's linked spiritual and economic concerns, like those of More and her fictional counterparts in the tracts, grow from a conviction that industry, proper employment, is the route to social harmony. He writes:

And how are the Ends both of Religion and Government to be answered, but by the System of universal Commerce? – Commerce, I mean, in the large and extensive Signification of that Word; Commerce, as it implies a general System for the *useful* Employment of our Time; as it exercises the particular Genius and Abilities of Mankind in some Way or other, either of Body or Mind, in mental or corporeal Labour, and so as to make Self-Interest and Social coincide. And in pursuing this Plan, it answers all the great Ends both of Religion and Government; it creates social Relations, it enables Men to discharge their Duty in those Relations, and it serves as a cement to connect together the Religious and Civil interests of Mankind. It is a Friend to both, when rightly understood, and is befriended by them.

(1774: 10–11)

In Tucker's expounding of the providential scheme, economic freedom must be found conformable to civil and divine authority, and the excellence of the commercial model as it evolves is that it extends productivity down to the humblest in society. In doing so, it ensures conformity while promoting well-being. In his writings on the evils of drink and in his various proposals for curbing what he saw as 'the first and capital disadvantage' of Britain, that is 'the Want of Subordination in the lower Class of People', which 'is attended with dreadful Consequences, both in a Commercial and a Moral View', Tucker's concern was the transformation of idleness into conformable productivity (1750: 36ff.).

Significantly for the high place More will allocate to women in stimulating industry, Tucker believed, and unusually so for his time, that a conformable productivity required women to play a more active role in the economy. He notes, for example, how among the beneficial effects of mechanisation in the Birmingham factories is the expansion of job opportunities for women (1757: 23); elsewhere he sees that female debauchery is the direct consequence of men filling positions which more properly belong to women (1750: 130–1). Like More, too, he advocated methods by which the middle might police the education and amusements of the bottom of society and so redefine lower-class identity. To promote thrift, religious observance, and family values, he proposes the erection of 'Courts' 'with the Title of Guardians of the Morals of the manufacturing poor' (1750: 53–4). Though conceived on a grander scale, their design and suggested system of rewards might be compared to the actual jurisdiction of the Mendip Women's Clubs and Friendly Societies run on near-regimental lines by Hannah and Martha More. Similarly, Tucker saw in the charity school system an opportunity for social amelioration and modest improvement which would also serve to preserve the necessary distinctions between ranks:

Nor can the Managers of these Charities have other Views than that of enabling these Children to get their Bread in the

meanest, the most laborious, and the least gainful Im-
ployments that belong to Society. . . . And most undoubtedly, if any of them should hereafter be able to rise in the
World by such means, as would promote the Interests of the
Public, as well as serve themselves; they ought to be at full
Liberty to do it: They ought to be permitted, nay encouraged
to grow *rich*, according to their Rank and Station, and in
proportion to their *Diligence*.

(1766: 19–20)

This is the concluding message of many of More's tracts, too,
where minimal schooling and basic literacy are seen as women's
specific contribution to promoting social conformity and ordered
productivity within the economy. Thus Mrs Jones, in *The Sunday
School* (May 1797), counters Farmer Hoskins's fears that a literate
workman will challenge the authority of his master:

> 'Now the whole extent of learning which we intend to give
> the poor, is only to enable them to read the Bible, a book in
> which duty is explained, every doctrine brought into prac-
> tice, and the highest truths made level to the meanest
> understanding. The knowledge of that book, and its practi-
> cal influence on the heart, is the best security you can have,
> both for the industry and obedience of your servants.'

More stands at the confluence of several economic discourses.
The daily practicalities of her household management have their
roots in an earlier tradition of domestic manuals, like Elizabeth
Moxon's *English Housewifry* (9th edn, 1764) and Charlotte
Mason's *The Ladies' Assistant for Regulating and Supplying the Table*
(7th edn, 1793). But the national importance which she attributes
to her model derives from a conscious feminisation of various
elements in the public representation of the moral and political
economy. Here More stands within an enlarged female tradition
which includes Sarah Trimmer's *Œconomy of Charity* (1787; 1801),
Priscilla Wakefield's *Reflections on the Present Condition of the Female
Sex; with suggestions for its improvement* (1798), shorter pieces like
Mary Lamb's 'On Needle-Work' (1815), and eventually Jane
Marcet's *Conversations on Political Economy* (1816) and Harriet
Martineau's *Illustrations of Political Economy* (1832).

Trimmer suggests just how empowering charitable activities
can be for women in proving 'the importance of the Female Sex in
society' (1801: 1.xii). Commenting on a scheme implemented in
St Albans to supply food to the poor at reduced prices, she

observes: 'When it is considered that a charity, which so materially contributes to the relief of betwixt *eight and nine hundred families* is entirely managed by ONE LADY, will not every Lady . . . feel herself competent to the execution of a similar plan, upon a smaller scale?' (Trimmer 1801: 2.87–8) More's domestic militant Mrs Jones speaks for women's vital role in 'restoring the good old management'. Prudent housekeeping and domestic vigilance, it is suggested in *The Cottage Cook*, particularly in Mrs Jones's justification of the necessity for sometimes turning public informer against dishonest tradesmen, demonstrate the link between the kitchen economy and the nation's well-being. The connection is extended when Mrs Jones, the merchant's widow, informs the village squire that she is herself a manufacturer, providing 'an excellent staple commodity', 'GOOD WIVES FOR WORKING MEN'. Wakefield's detailed proposals for women's rights to jobs and professions at all levels of society are based, she maintains, on Adam Smith's pronouncement 'that every individual is a burthen upon the society to which he belongs, who does not contribute his share of productive labour for the good of the whole.' If productive labour is 'a moral excellence in one rational being [then, she asserts, it] deserves the same estimation in another.' (Wakefield 1798: 1; and 68) But her arguments in favour of extending women's professional opportunities and their share of the job market clearly draw her closer to Tucker than to Smith.

Analogy is endemic to economic thinking. According to the modern American economist Donald McCloskey, one of the best reasons we have for believing in the Law of Demand is analogy (1986: 60). Economists persuade us analogically, by telling stories. Hannah More understands this. 'Restoring the good old management' is Mrs Jones's mission, and by extension her author More's, too. Both use the moralised particulars of their homely vignettes to derive the larger social organisation analogically from the domestic model: 'May all who read this account of Mrs Jones "go and do likewise"', her narrator instructs. More's constructed family is a 'well-governed society', an enterprise whose productive centre is woman; equally for More, home economics stands mid-way between the providential ordering of the universe and the regulation of the state. The temporary strength of More's rhetoric derives from its skilful redeployment of women's own newly empowered borrowed tongue. Moreover, analogy, like metaphor, is no mere 'verbal trick', but, in I. A. Richards's definition, 'a borrowing between and intercourse of thoughts, a transaction between contexts'. In other words, its basis is economic – a matter of 'mutually advantageous exchange' (McCloskey 1986:77). As a propagandist and a woman More understood the productive potential of exchange. In the short term at least, it makes of her muscular philanthropy something more than a dream of female power.

Note

1. The Repository tracts are short and were issued in various forms making page citation an irregular method of identification. Consequently, in referring to individual tracts, I give publication dates but not page references, except where material cited is from later collected editions of More's work.

References

Butler, M. (1975). *Jane Austen and the War of Ideas*. Oxford, Clarendon Press, rev. edn., 1987.

Gilbert, S.M. and Susan Gubar, (1979). *The Madwoman in the Attic: the Woman Writer and the Nineteenth-Century Female Imagination*. New Haven and London, Yale University Press.

de Gouges, O. (1989). *The Rights of Woman*, trans. Val Stevenson. London, Pythia Press.

Hutcheson, F. (1755). *A System of Moral Philosophy, in Three Books*. 2 vols., London.

Kaplan, C. (1985). 'Pandora's Box: Subjectivity, Class, and Sexuality in Socialist Feminist Criticism', in *Making a Difference: Feminist Literary Criticism*, ed. Gayle Greene and Coppélia Kahn. London and New York, Methuen, pp. 146–76.

Kirkham, M. (1983). *Jane Austen, Feminism, and Fiction*. Brighton, Harvester Press.

McCloskey, D.N. (1986). *The Rhetoric of Economics*. Brighton, Harvester Press.

More, H. (1799). *Strictures on the Modern System of Female Education. With a view of the principles and conduct prevalent among women of rank and fortune*. 2 vols., London.

—— (1818). *The Works of Hannah More*. 18 vols., London.

Myers, M. (1982). 'Reform or Ruin: "A Revolution in Female Manners"', *Studies in Eighteenth-Century Culture*, 11, ed. Harry C. Payne. Madison, Wisconsin, University of Wisconsin Press, pp. 199–216.

—— (1986). 'Hannah More's Tracts for the Times: Social Fiction and Female Ideology', in *Fetter'd or Free: British Women Novelists 1670–1815*, ed. Mary Anne Schofield and Cecilia Macheski. Athens, Ohio, Ohio University Press, pp. 264–84.

Newman, G. (1975). 'Anti-French Propaganda and British Liberal Nationalism in the Early Nineteenth Century: suggestions toward a general interpretation', *Victorian Studies*, 18, 385–418.

Outram, D. (1987). 'Le Langage Mâle de la Vertu: Women and the Discourse of the French Revolution', in *The Social History of Language*, ed. Peter Burke and Roy Porter. Cambridge, Cambridge University Press, pp. 120–35.

Pocock, J.G.A., (1975). *The Machiavellian Moment: Florentine Political Thought and the Atlantic Republican Tradition*. Princeton, New Jersey, Princeton University Press.

—— (1983). 'Cambridge Paradigms and Scotch Philosophers: a study of the relations between the civic humanist and the civic jurisprudential interpretation of eighteenth-century social thought', in *Wealth and Virtue: the Shaping of Political Economy in the Scottish Enlightenment*, ed. Istvan Hont and Michael Ignatieff. Cambridge, Cambridge University Press, pp. 235–52.

—— (1985). *Virtue, Commerce, and Society: Essays on Political Thought and History, Chiefly in the Eighteenth Century*. Cambridge, Cambridge University Press.

Poovey, M. (1984). *The Proper Lady and the Woman Writer: Ideology as Style in the Works of Mary Wollstonecraft, Mary Shelley, and Jane Austen*. Chicago and London, University of Chicago Press.

Riley, D. (1988). *'Am I That Name?' Feminism and the Category of 'Women' in History*. Basingstoke, Hants, and London, Macmillan.

Roberts, A. ed. (1859). *Mendip Annals: or a Narrative of the Charitable Labours of Hannah and Martha More in their Neighbourhood. Being the Journal of Martha More*. 2nd edn., London.

Roberts, W. ed. (1834). *Memoirs of the Life and Correspondence of Mrs Hannah More*. 2nd edn., 4 vols., London.

Rowbotham, S. (1973). *Hidden from History: 300 Years of Women's Oppression and the Fight Against It*. 3rd edn., London, Pluto Press, 1977.

Schnorrenberg, B.B. (1980). 'The Eighteenth-Century Englishwoman', in *The Women of England from Anglo-Saxon Times to the Present*, ed. Barbara Kanner. London, Mansell, pp. 183–228.

Scott, J.W. (1988). *Gender and the Politics of History*. New York, Columbia University Press.

Smith, A. (1976a). *An Inquiry into the Nature and Causes of the Wealth of Nations*, ed. R.H. Campbell, A.S. Skinner, and W.B. Todd. 2 vols., Oxford, Clarendon Press.

—— (1976b). *The Theory of Moral Sentiments*, ed. D.D. Raphael and A.L. Macfie. Oxford, Clarendon Press.

Spinney, G.H. (1939–40). 'Cheap Repository Tracts: Hazard and Marshall Edition', *The Library*, 4th Series, 20, 295–340.

Steuart, J. (1767). *An Inquiry into the Principles of Political Œconomy: Being an Essay on the Science of Domestic Policy in Free Nations*. 2 vols., London.

Thompson, D. (1984). *The Chartists*. London, Temple Smith.

Thompson, H. (1838). *The Life of Hannah More: with notices of her sisters.* London.

Todd, J. (1988). *Feminist Literary History: A Defence.* Cambridge, Polity Press.

Trimmer, S. (1788–9). *The Family Magazine; or a Repository of Religious Instruction, and Rational Amusement. Designed to counteract the pernicious tendency of immoral books, &c. which have circulated of late years among the inferior classes of people, to the obstruction of their improvement in religion and morality.* London.

—— (1801). *The Oeconomy of Charity; or an Address to Ladies; adapted to the Present State of Charitable Institutions in England: with a particular view to the cultivation of religious principles, among the lower orders of people.* 2 vols, London.

[Tucker, J.] (1750). *A Brief Essay on the Advantages and Disadvantages which respectively attend France and Great Britain, with regard to Trade. With some Proposals for removing the Principal Disadvantages of Great Britain. In a New Method.* 2nd edn., London.

Tucker, J. (1757). *Instructions for Travellers.* London.

—— (1766). *A Sermon preached in the Parish-Church of Christ-Church, London, on Wednesday May the 7th, 1766 . . .* London.

—— (1774). *Four Tracts, together with Two Sermons.* Gloucester.

Wakefield, P. (1798). *Reflections on the Present Condition of the Female Sex; with suggestions for its improvement.* London.

Wollstonecraft, M. (1975). *A Vindication of the Rights of Woman,* ed. Miriam Brody Kramnick. Harmondsworth, Penguin.

Woolf, V. (1945). *A Room of One's Own.* Harmondsworth, Penguin.

—— (1977). *Three Guineas.* Harmondsworth, Penguin.

Selina Young

4

Gender in revolution: Edmund Burke and Mary Wollstonecraft

Tom Furniss

I

Cora Kaplan argues that instabilities of class and gender opened up by republican and liberal political philosophy at the end of the eighteenth century became the central concern of a range of bourgeois discourses in the nineteenth century. In the novel, for example,

> The language of class . . . obsessively inscribes a class system whose divisions and boundaries are at once absolute and impregnable and in constant danger of dissolution. Often in these narratives it is a woman whose class identity is at risk or problematic; the woman and her sexuality are a condensed and displaced representation of the dangerous instabilities of class and gender identity for both sexes.[1]

This meant that a notion of 'true womanhood' had to be constructed which was at once differentiated from masculinity and from subordinated races and classes: 'The difference between men and women in the ruling class had to be written so that a slippage into categories reserved for lesser humanities could be averted'. At the same time, however, patriarchy's need to subordinate women by ascribing to them a 'primitive' propensity for passion means that 'The line between the primitive and the degraded feminine is a thin one' (p. 167). Women of the ruling class are thus given an irresolvably contradictory meaning: they at once epitomise that class's distinctive quality and threaten to subvert it from within. In the present article, I want to revise Kaplan's suggestion that such instabilities of class and gender were opened up by radical and liberal thought in the 1790s by showing how they are intrinsic to Edmund Burke's attempt to institute bourgeois capitalism in the second half of the eighteenth century. We will see that these inbuilt instabilities in Burke's discursive project simply get foregrounded or dramatised in the textual struggle between Burke and his liberal and radical antagonists. In order to show this, I will examine Burke's texts from perspectives opened up by Mary Wollstonecraft's perceptive critique of them and then turn that critique back onto Wollstonecraft's own texts. In this way, it may prove possible to understand some of the dynamics of the way Wollstonecraft's treatment of aesthetics, gender and politics is crucially implicated in the political positions it attempts to overturn. Thus, the present article works to modify Kaplan's suggestion that Wollstonecraft's bourgeois feminism has to be understood as a complex and contradictory response to Rousseau by arguing that Burke is a still more powerful interlocutor whose texts paradoxically empower Wollstonecraft's thought even as she seeks to displace them.

II

Burke's narrative of the events at Versailles on 5–6 October 1789, which is often said to form the central scene of his account of the Revolution in *Reflections on the Revolution in France* (1790),[2] seeks to exploit, but is also deeply troubled by, instabilities of gender and class in the revolutionary moment. In order to investigate why this should be so, I want to take up Wollstonecraft's insight, in *A Vindication of the Rights of Men* (1790), that Burke's politics in *Reflections* are grounded in the aesthetics developed in his mid-century treatise, *A Philosophical Enquiry into the Origin of our Ideas of the Sublime and Beautiful* (1757/59).[3] In briefly examining Burke's *Enquiry*, I want to single out that aspect which Wollstonecraft stresses – that there is an explicit sexual politics in this treatise, and that its aesthetic categories are constituted as, and help perpetuate, conventional eighteenth-century gender distinctions.

The *Enquiry* is written explicitly and exclusively from a male perspective, and we will see that the way it theorises the sublime's 'delightful horror' – which arises in a moment of self-preservation in face of apparent danger – makes it by definition an experience available to men rather than to women (since it is a 'masculine' response to the debilitating effects of 'feminine' beauty). Burke's distinction between the sublime and the beautiful is grounded in the commonplace eighteenth-century discrimination between the passions which belong to self-preservation and those which belong to society (see *Enquiry*, pp. 38–41), but although 'society' is said to include society in general (the pleasurable concourse with both men and women), the bulk of Burke's argument makes it plain that beauty is experienced most fully in men's sexual perception of women. For Burke, a woman's particular beauty is that which makes the difference between human procreation and the 'lust' which 'is evident in brutes, whose passions are more unmixed, and which pursue their purposes more directly than ours' (p. 42). Human sexual relationships differ from those of the 'brutes' in that the 'only distinction they observe with regard to their mates, is that of sex' (p. 42). Beauty in women is a *social* quality because it 'direct[s] and heighten[s] the appetite which [man] has in common with all other animals', and thus transforms momentary and indiscriminate lust by encouraging a man to enter into a more permanent relation with a particular woman:

> The object therefore of this mixed passion which we call love, is the *beauty* of the *sex*. Men are carried to the sex in general, as it is the sex, and by the common law of nature; but they are attached to particulars by personal *beauty*.
>
> (p. 42)

Thus, beauty becomes that extra something which raises human beings (or should we read it as women here?) above the level of the 'brutes'.

Although Burke admits that 'both sexes are undoubtedly capable of beauty', it is the female which is capable 'of the greatest' (p. 98). However, the quality that is most admired in men is one quite different to that celebrated in women:

> if beauty in our own species was annexed to use, men would be much more lovely than women; and strength and agility would be considered as the only beauties. But to call strength by the name of beauty, to have but one denomination for the qualities of a Venus and Hercules, so totally different in

almost all respects, is surely a strange confusion of ideas, or
abuse of words.

(p. 106)

In fact, 'feminine' beauty becomes the very antithesis of 'masculine' strength:

> this quality, where it is highest in the female sex, almost
> always carries with it an idea of weakness and imperfection.
> Women are very sensible of this; for which reason, they learn
> to lisp, to totter in their walk, to counterfeit weakness, and
> even sickness. In all this, they are guided by nature. Beauty
> in distress is much the most affecting beauty.

(p. 110)

Burke's treatise therefore reinforces what it presents as natural
gender divisions – which form, in fact, the most compelling
instance of the difference between the sublime and the beautiful:

> There is a wide difference between admiration and love. The
> sublime, which is the cause of the former, always dwells on
> great objects, and terrible; the latter on small ones, and
> pleasing; we submit to what we admire, but we love what
> submits to us; in one case we are forced, in the other we are
> flattered into compliance.

(pp. 113–14)

The sexual politics of these power relations – of submission and of
being submitted to – seem clear enough, but I want to argue that
we need to read this gendering of aesthetic categories in
mid-eighteenth-century England in terms of class and national
distinctions as well as sexual difference. As Kaplan puts it,

> Masculinity and femininity do not appear in cultural dis-
> course, any more than they do in mental life, as pure binary
> forms at play. They are always, already, ordered and broken
> up through other social and cultural terms, other categories
> of difference. . . . To understand how gender and class – to
> take two categories only – are articulated together transforms
> our analysis of each of them.

('Subjectivity, class and sexuality', p. 148)

I want to suggest that class and gender are articulated together
in mid eighteenth-century England through its ubiquitous concern with the implications and effects of 'luxury'. John Sekora has
shown that the notion of luxury – inherited through the Bible and

the literature of Greece and Rome – is one of the essentially contested concepts of eighteenth-century political thought in England. Defenders of the aristocratic order frequently attacked the up-and-coming bourgeoisie for its 'luxury', while the apologists for the bourgeoisie used the same loaded term in its criticism of the traditional ruling class.[4] Both classes agreed, however, in condemning the 'luxury' of France's *ancien régime* and of the 'lower orders' in Britain (Sekora, pp. 90–98 and 37). Luxury was universally condemned because it was held to initiate a physiological dissolution of the individual body so contagious that it inevitably led to the dissolution of the body politic. Writing in the *London Magazine* in September 1754 (three years before Burke's *Enquiry* was first published), 'Civis' warns that

> Amongst the many reigning vices of the present age none have risen to a greater height than that fashionable one of luxury, and few require a more immediate suppression, as it not only enervates the people, and debauches their morals, but also destroys their substance.
>
> (quoted by Sekora, p. 65)

The political consequences of this are spelt out by another correspondent in the January issue of 1756, who claims that the increase of luxury 'threaten[s] the undermining of our constitution and the downfall of our state' (quoted by Sekora, p. 65). Of particular interest here is that luxury was typically associated with effeminacy and figured as feminine. Sekora points out that early Jewish and Christian commentators stressed that Eve's fall and temptation of Adam was a sin of luxury (p. 24), that writers such as Cato and Tertullian condemned the 'vice' and 'extravagance' of women (pp. 40 and 49), and that 'almost all personifications of luxury are feminine' (p. 44).

Burke's representation of beauty draws on contemporary figurations of luxury and of the feminine as at once irresistibly alluring and physically and politically dangerous. When in the presence of 'such objects as excite love and complacency', the observer is affected 'with an inward sense of melting and langour' (*Enquiry*, p. 149). Given this, Burke suggests that 'it is almost impossible not to conclude, that beauty acts by relaxing the solids of the whole system' (pp. 149–50), and adduces as evidence 'that manner of expression so common in all times and in all countries, of being softened, relaxed, enervated, dissolved, melted away by pleasure' (p. 150). But if we might be misled into thinking that Burke is celebrating the peculiar sensation that beauty produces, it is worth juxtaposing these comments with an earlier description of the effects of relaxation, which

> not only disables the members from performing their functions, but carries away the vigorous tone of fibre which is requisite for carrying on the natural and necessary secretions. At the same time . . . in this languid inactive state, the nerves are more liable to the most horrid convulsions, than when they are sufficiently braced and strengthened. Melancholy, dejection, despair, and often self-murder, is the consequence of the gloomy view we take of things in this relaxed state of the body.
>
> (p. 135)

Burke's 'antidote' to this contagious and debilitating state produced by beauty is labour:

> The best remedy for all these evils is exercise or *labour*; and labour is a surmounting of *difficulties*, an exertion of the contracting power of the muscles; and as such resembles pain, which consists in tension or contraction, in every thing but degree.
>
> (p. 135)

By making the pain of common labour analogous to 'the exercise of the finer parts of the system' produced by terror (p. 136), Burke makes the self-preservation effected by labour here into an exemplary instance of the sublime. Thus, the sublime's importance is that it acts as a 'masculine' antidote to the beautiful itself – which needs to be resisted because it is at once the primary vehicle of civilisation and that which perpetually threatens to undermine it.

In her perceptive reading of Burke's aesthetics, Frances Ferguson suggests that 'the question we must ask of Burke's *Enquiry* is what is tyrannical about the beautiful, or, why must it be resisted? For we cannot understand the force of the sublime unless we understand what it is an alternative to.'[5] In Ferguson's reading, Burke's beautiful is that which actually poses a more dangerous threat to self and society than the sublime:

> For the beautiful . . . figures in the *Enquiry* not just as the domestic and social or as that which submits to us, it is also the deceptive *par excellence*. In the case of the sublime, Burke

says, 'we are forced', while with the beautiful, 'we are flattered into compliance'.

(p. 75)

Ferguson's discussion of one of the *Enquiry*'s examples of the effects of the beautiful is particularly significant for my present purpose: 'the Trojan War itself', she notes, referring to Burke's observation that Homer makes his Greeks sublime and his Trojans beautiful, 'appears in illustration of beauty's disastrous consequences not only for the body but for the body politic as well' (p. 75). Helen's beauty is 'fatal' (*Enquiry*, pp. 171–72) to the Trojans (who present an exemplary warning to all political states) not merely because her residence in Troy draws the avenging Greeks but, Ferguson argues, because 'the danger in beauty is that its appearance of weakness does not prevent its having an effect, which is always that of robbing us of our vigilance and recreating us in its own image'. Ferguson concludes that

> After the beautiful has been joined with physical and political entropy issuing in death, the importance of the sublime in exciting the passions of self-preservation becomes apparent. For although the sublime inspires us with fear of our death, the beautiful leads us towards death without our awareness.
>
> (p. 76)

III

If the *Enquiry* can thus be seen as being centrally concerned with maintaining what it presents as the politically crucial distinction between masculinity and femininity, the French Revolution confronts Burke with a curious problem in that he is forced to defend and eulogise a traditional order in France which seems the very embodiment of the beautiful and to condemn a revolution which could be seen as the sublime antidote to an institutionalised luxury. Such contradictions are perhaps most powerfully at work in the passages in *Reflections* where Burke brings the *ancien régime* and the Revolution into dramatic confrontation – his narrative of the events at Versailles on 5–6 October 1789. In order to understand what follows, it will be useful here to quote from a recent account of these events:

> On 5 October women gathered before the Hotel de Ville demanding bread: this was quite normal. Getting no satisfaction the cry was raised – by whom? – that they should make

their way to Versailles to appeal to the king. Several thousands set out, gathering numbers as they went. . . . At four o'clock in the afternoon the Municipal Council authorised La Fayette to move off with the National Guard, and now there appeared for the first time a definite objective: the king was to be brought back to Paris. With a mixed body of National Guards and others La Fayette set out. . . . That evening the main body of the Parisians arrived, settled down for the night as best they could or ranged about the streets of Versailles and the courts of the palace. At early dawn on the next day a few hundred of the demonstrators found a way into the palace, slaughtered some of the royal bodyguard whom they encountered and penetrated nearly to the queen's apartments before they were repulsed.

Morning saw serried masses in the courtyard before the palace, now with one cry, 'To Paris!' . . . In the afternoon of 6 October the triumphal procession set out on the muddy march back to Paris – National Guards armed and royal bodyguard disarmed, wagons laden with corn and flour lumbering, market men and women straggling along . . . La Fayette riding alongside the carriage bearing the royal family, also beside them the heads of two of the Royal Guards on pikes . . . and trudging along in the rapidly falling twilight the dark shapes of thousands of nameless Parisians. At ten o'clock . . . the royal family . . . at last reached the Tuileries . . . and camped down in hurriedly cleared rooms as best they could for the night.[6]

It is important to realise that Burke's version of these events was prompted not by the events themselves but by Richard Price's representation of them in *A Discourse on the Love of Our Country* (1789) as a heroic climax to the people's demand for liberty in which they led their king 'in triumph' and forced him to surrender himself to his subjects.[7] In looking at Burke's sustained attempt to deflate this 'triumph', I want to concentrate especially on the way questions of gender and of the role of women are both central to his rhetorical strategies and symptomatic of the internal contradictions of his reaction against the Revolution.

As in many other accounts of the Versailles episode, women play an active part in Burke's narrative. In describing the procession back to Paris, for example, Burke depicts the royal family being

conducted to the capital of their kingdom . . . amidst the
horrid yells, and shrilling screams, and frantic dances, and
infamous contumelies, and all the unutterable abominations
of the furies of hell, in the abused shape of the vilest of
women.

(*Reflections*, pp. 164–65)

Far from being a 'triumph', Burke suggests that this

was (unless we have been strangely deceived) a spectacle
more resembling a procession of American savages . . . after
some of their murders called victories, and leading into
hovels hung round with scalps, their captives, overpowered
with the scoffs and buffets of women as ferocious as
themselves, much more than it resembled the triumphal
pomp of a civilised martial nation.

(p. 159)

Burke presents such violations of 'proper' gender roles and
behavioural patterns as both endemic to and emblematic of a
general breakdown of political order:

The Assembly, their organ, acts before [the people] the farce
of deliberation with as little decency as liberty. They act like
the comedians of a fair before a riotous audience; they act
amidst the tumultuous cries of a mixed mob of ferocious
men, and of women lost to shame, who, according to their
insolent fancies, direct, control, applaud, explode them; and
sometimes mix and take their seats amongst them; domi-
neering over them with a strange mixture of servile petu-
lance and proud presumptuous authority. As they have
inverted order in all things, the gallery is in place of the
house.

(p. 161)[8]

Burke therefore presents a series of vivid images in which the
Revolution is shown to have broken loose from civilising constraints. In each of these images women are depicted as having
abandoned their femininity (or at least their traditional roles) and
their modesty (they are 'lost to shame'), and to have thereby
blurred the distinctions between themselves and the savage or
the inhuman.

Burke's representation of these events enables him to juxta-
pose and contrast the terror of revolution (epitomised by these

various gatherings of terrifying women) with the vulnerable beauty of the ancien regime (epitomised by the French queen):

> History will record, that on the morning of the 6th of October 1789, the king and queen of France, after a day of confusion, alarm, dismay, and slaughter, lay down, under the pledged security of public faith, to indulge nature in a few hours of respite, and troubled melancholy repose. From this sleep the queen was first startled by the voice of the centinel at her door, who cried out to her, to save herself by flight – that this was the last proof of fidelity he could give – that they were upon him, and he was dead. Instantly he was cut down. A band of cruel ruffians and assassins, reeking with his blood, rushed into the chamber of the queen, and pierced with an hundred strokes of bayonets and poniards the bed, from whence this persecuted woman had but just time to fly almost naked . . . to seek refuge at the feet of a king and husband, not secure of his own life for a moment.
>
> (p. 164)

Burke 'confesses' to his nominal addressee that the intensity of his response to the queen's experiences (as he represents them) derives from her social rank and particularly from her gender:

> I confess to you, Sir, that the exalted rank of the persons suffering, and particularly the sex, the beauty, and the amiable qualities [of the French queen] . . . instead of being a subject of exultation, adds not a little to my sensibility on that most melancholy occasion.
>
> (p. 168)

This emphasis on the queen's beauty is continued in Burke's description of his own encounter with Marie Antoinette at Versailles in 1773:

> It is now sixteen or seventeen years since I saw the queen of France, then the dauphiness, at Versailles; and surely never lighted on this orb, which she hardly seemed to touch, a more delightful vision. I saw her just above the horizon, decorating and cheering the elevated sphere she just began to move in, – glittering like the morning star, full of life, and splendour, and joy. Oh! What a revolution! and what an

heart must I have, to contemplate without emotion that elevation and that fall!

(p. 169)

By thus dwelling on the *effect* of Marie Antoinette's beauty rather than attempting to describe it, Burke imitates Homer's evocation of Helen's beauty in the *Iliad* – a literary device which Burke praises in the *Enquiry* as an exemplary instance of the beautiful (pp. 171–72). But while the *Enquiry* had devalued the beautiful (seeing it as something to be feared and resisted), these passages in *Reflections* clearly attempt to exploit an image of beauty in distress and to distinguish between the 'delightful horror' of the true sublime and the sheer terror and brutality of the Revolution (a distinction which is, as we will see, a problematic one in Burke's aesthetics).

But given that Burke seems to realise the political danger of his notion of the beautiful in 1757–59, it is curious that he should defend it in *Reflections* – where Paris and Marie Antoinette seem figured as contemporary equivalents of Homer's Troy and Helen. It seems clear that, despite his eulogies, France's *ancien régime* is far from embodying Burke's political and aesthetic ideals – its system seems, in fact, according to the principles developed in the *Enquiry*, precisely of a kind most calculated to endanger the political organism. In attempting to understand some of the complex motivations which force Burke into such a problematic position, it is important to realise, as C.B. Macpherson has argued, that Burke attacks the Revolution and defends the *ancien régime* not because he is concerned to uphold traditional institutions and customs in Britain for their own sake, but because they offer a more secure way than revolution of introducing bourgeois capitalist practices.[9] But I would suggest that the peculiar rhetorical energy of *Reflections* arises through the contradictions which this strategy involves Burke in, since he is driven to both defend the *ancien régime* in order to repudiate the Revolution and present it to his English readers as a salutary example of the inevitable consequences of luxury in the ruling class.

IV

Burke seeks to impress on his readers that the 'atrocities' enacted at Versailles represent a revolution not only in politics but in manners: 'the most important of all revolutions, which may be dated from that day' is 'a revolution in sentiments, manners, and moral opinions' (p. 175). His lamentation over the effects of such a revolution are well-known and revealing:

> All the pleasing illusions, which made power gentle, and obedience liberal, which . . . incorporated into politics the sentiments which beautify and soften private society, are to be dissolved by this new conquering empire of light and reason. All the decent drapery of life is to be rudely torn off. All the super-added ideas, furnished from the wardrobe of a moral imagination, which the heart owns, and the understanding ratifies, as necessary to cover the defects of our naked shivering nature, and to raise it to dignity in our own estimation, are to be exploded as a ridiculous, absurd, and antiquated fashion.
>
> (p. 171)[10]

In *Reflections*, then, beauty has become less the effect of smooth skin and a gradually varying line epitomised by the exposed neck and breasts of a 'beautiful' woman (*Enquiry*, p. 115) than precisely that which would 'cover the defects of our naked shivering nature' and so disguise the basic equality of human beings. Following Rousseau, who claimed to have 'demolished the petty lies of mankind; [and to have] dared to strip man's nature naked',[11] radical discourse of the 1790s makes the *exposure* of institutional defects hidden by costume, customs and language a political imperative. Habitual manners and customs thus become one of the aspects of traditional society which is most threatened by revolutionary violence and most valued by Burke – perhaps because they form one of the most effective means of pre-empting rational enquiry. But Burke's equation of habit and custom with the beautiful in order to form the supplement *par excellence* of civilised society conveniently 'forgets' the desensitising effects of habit and custom which are identified in the *Enquiry*. In that earlier text, habit and custom are seen as antithetical to both the sublime and the beautiful since 'the effect of constant use is to make all things of whatever kind entirely unaffecting' (*Enquiry*, p. 104).

There are a number of ways, however, in which Burke's text empowers a radical critique of the aristocratic system. That extra something which constitutes beauty, fosters love and promotes society has been exposed (by the revolutionaries? by Burke's text?) as a set of 'pleasing *illusions*' susceptible to being dissolved or torn away. The stripping of the queen and the stripping of aristocratic society thus become figures for one another, and 'the defects of our naked shivering nature' can be seen as both figurative and literal:

> On this scheme of things, a king is but a man; a queen is but a woman; a woman is but an animal; and an animal not of the highest order. All homage paid to the sex in general as such, and without distinct views, is to be regarded as romance and folly.
>
> (*Reflections*, p. 171)

If the decent drapery of life seems to soften but also maintain often brutal hierarchies, the disrobing intrusions of revolutionary thought therefore reveal for Burke not simply an anatomical equality between ranks but a frightening difference between the sexes. In Burke, revolution leaves the king a man, but the queen's 'fall' – from queen to woman, to animal, to animal not of the highest order – is much more precipitous and disturbing. Burke's unspoken assumption seems to be that clothes make the woman – that a woman is always in need of supplementation in order to raise her nature from beneath to beyond the human. Yet the interrelated social system of supplements – codes, manners, customs, costumes – which guarantees both femininity and society is at the same time that which points to their vulnerability. But although Marie Antoinette's 'fall' becomes an analogue for that of the *ancien régime*, it is not immediately clear why the removal of her clothes should not simply reveal her as a woman rather than transforming her from more to less than human. This 'fall' is precipitated within and by Burke's text – for if she is stripped within *Reflections*, it is there too that she is at once eulogised as the epitome of beauty and made into a kind of beast. The exposure of the queen instantaneously reduces her from the most elevated example of those particulars of personal beauty which inspire love to a body which displays those generalities of sexual anatomy which rouse a lust akin to that of the brutes.

That Marie Antoinette could be treated in this way in France suggests to Burke that

> the age of chivalry is gone. . . . Never, never more, shall we behold that generous loyalty to rank and sex, that proud submission, that dignified obedience, that subordination of

the heart, which kept alive, even in servitude itself, the spirit
of an exalted freedom.

(p. 170)

But although servitude to women might form part of the chivalric
code, it is quite at odds with the sexual politics of Burke's *Enquiry*,
which suggests that 'we submit to what we admire, but we love
what submits to us' (p. 113). In the *Enquiry*, submission to women
would be dangerous folly since the love which women are
supposed to inspire has debilitating effects on the masculine
physical, psychic and political economy. In *Reflections*, by contrast, submission to rank and sex is said to have once been 'the
nurse of manly sentiment and heroic enterprise', inspiring
'courage whilst it mitigated ferocity' (p. 170). In 1790, then,
chivalry is presented as that code of behaviour which harmonises
two aesthetic impulses which were considered incompatible in
1757–59 – where, in the presence of the sublime, 'the qualities of
beauty [lie] either dead and unoperative; or at most exerted to
mollify the rigour and sternness of the terror' (*Enquiry*, p. 157).
What emerges in *Reflections*, therefore, is that members of a
chivalric society experience, in 'that proud submission, that
dignified obedience', an oxymoronic and necessarily precarious
conflation of the sublime and the beautiful. Heroic deeds, he now
claims, are done *for* the beautiful rather than in retreat from it.

V

One of the ways in which recent criticism has tried to account for
the ambiguities and contradictions which surface in Burke's text
in the passages we have been examining is to suggest that they
are symptomatic of a partially unresolved oedipus complex in the
author. Such a reading, which originates with Isaac Kramnick, is
elaborated by Ronald Paulson: 'we see Burke opposing a vigor-
ous ("active"), unprincipled, rootless masculine sexuality, unleashed and irrepressible, against a gentle aristocratic family,
patriarchal and based on bonds of love'. Paulson argues that this
psycho-ideological motive force is combined with a use of

> extremely conventional literary elements . . . which derive
> from the polemics of the English Civil War and its aftermath,
> in which religious enthusiasm leads to the unleashing of
> sexual drives and/or the overturning of government.

Burke's dramatic scene conflates these sexual and political impulses:

> When you strip the queen, you expose the principle of equality, but you also prove your masculinity in relation to the king (the 'father' of his people . . .). You pierce the queen's bed 'with an hundred strokes of bayonets and poniards' as a surrogate for the queen herself.[12]

It is difficult to know how one could confirm or deny such claims about the *origins* of these passages, but such readings might be used to stimulate discussions about the *structure* and the *effects* of Burke's treatment of the Versailles episode. Thus, Burke's text may be theorised in terms of the way images of the usurpation of a king and the rape of a queen might be expected to produce effects of terror. At the same time, however, it may also be read as an obscene joke shared by male protagonists over the abused sexuality of a woman. The latter reading responds to a different way of understanding the 'oedipal' symptoms which Kramnick traces:

> When the Jacobins uncover the particular nakedness of the queen, they discover the principle of equality. . . . Contemplating the naked queen is to penetrate all the mystery of the aristocratic principle. In discovering that in her nakedness Marie is but a mere woman, Burke joins Jacobin ideology to the crudity of an obscene joke. 'On this scheme of things, a king is but a man, a queen is but a woman; a woman is but an animal, and an animal not of the highest order'.
>
> (*Rage of Edmund Burke*, p. 153)

If to strip the queen is to 'expose the principle of equality' as well as to prove one's 'masculinity in relation to the king', the revolutionary urge combines the transgression of sexual and social boundaries. But since it is Burke's text which has the revolutionary 'mob' abuse the queen in this way (there is no reliable evidence to support Burke's account – he simply exaggerated contemporary reports), then this passage *produces* the revolutionary moment it claims simply to describe. The text which seems to recoil in horror from the Revolution turns out to linger voyeuristically over the woman it strips and actively to engage in the penetration of those mysteries which maintain aristocratic distinction.[13] *Reflections* therefore emerges as less a representation of the Revolution than the textual enactment of a revolution which it imagines and stages.

The celebration of Marie Antoinette therefore contains at least one moment which seems to unravel the delicate fabric which Burke weaves. Eulogy disturbingly takes on structural features which relate it to Freud's description of the dynamics of the 'dirty joke' – which typically involves obscenity and aggression towards a woman made unavailable through social constraints.[14] But if the effect of such a joke (which seeks to *expose* the woman's sexuality) depends, as Samuel Weber puts it, upon a 'voyeuristically inclined third person, "corrupted" (*bestochen*) by the promised "gift" of pleasure', then we might speculate on the way Burke's text positions its reader as that third person. The inhibited seduction of the woman is therefore redirected as an attempt to produce laughter in the reader – who becomes, as Weber puts it, the 'other man' who 'embodies the moral code and its interdictions'.[15] Burke's text may therefore work to establish a kind of complicity with his male radical readers through a shared aggression towards the female emblem of aristocratic society. For Weber, this shift from rivalry to complicity 'is also the structural "resolution" of the Oedipus complex'. But, as he says, 'whether this implies that the dirty joke is oedipal in structure, or conversely, that the Oedipus complex is a "dirty joke", is a question that will hardly permit a univocal response' (*Legend of Freud*, p. 108). It may be, then, that the reader's reaction to Burke's text – whether laughter, tears or anger – might be unforeseeable (this passage, like much of Burke's late rhetoric, prompted a wide variety of responses). Freud suggests that the teller of a joke always takes a certain risk that it might fail – that the burst of laughter which a joke aims to produce might not arise (*Jokes*, p. 204). In the present case, the opposite might occur: a tale intended to produce terror may unexpectedly work as a joke and so produce laughter. At the same time, Burke's horror story might unpredictably produce the delight associated with the sublime, since – as the *Enquiry* emphasises – 'whatever is qualified to cause terror, is a foundation capable of the sublime' (p. 131). Burke's text thus runs a double risk: terror may always have the potential to induce the sublime, while the sublime might always involve the risk of being received as a joke. For if, as Weber argues, the success or failure of a joke depends on momentarily breaching a set of shared social inhibitions and conventions, the joke is situated (like the sublime itself) in an ambiguous relation towards 'custom'.[16] At once dependent upon and disruptive of tradition – simultaneously, and unpredictably, 'reactionary' and 'revolutionary' – the joke therefore shares the political ambiguities of the 'carnival': 'In producing laughter', Weber writes,

> the joke thus represents a collective if temporary trans-gression of shared prohibitions. Jokes therefore are always specific to certain groups, which may be more or less extensive, but which are never simply universal.
>
> (p. 110)[17]

If Burke's 'oedipal scene' may function as a dirty joke that fails to provoke laughter, its politicised form and content yet allow for a revolutionary delight in the exposure of the queen and humili-ation of the king. And that delight depends precisely on the social and political inhibitions which Burke defends and which the bulk of his anecdote plays upon. For, as we have seen, it is the *institutional majesty* of the royal couple, and the consequent *untouchable beauty* of the queen, which form the particular social 'set' of this narrative: such customs and pleasing illusions condition both the reactionary horror and the 'revolutionary' delight. This is not, however, to speculate upon Burke's 'real' or 'covert' intentions; the present analysis suggests that it is this scene's *structure* and *effects* which are contradictory and unpre-dictable, regardless of what Burke was actually trying to do. Burke's scene may be read as both a tale of horror calculated to arouse indignation, and as a tendentious joke potentially arous-ing laughter. For, while neither effect can be calculated in advance, the forms and social conditions are the same for both.

Burke's ambiguous lamentation over the fate of Marie An-toinette may also be read as a joke which rouses not laughter but indignation. Weber asks an important question about jokes which has intriguing consequences for the way we might read Wollstonecraft's response to the passages in *Reflections* which accrue around the account of 5–6 October: 'In what way does he [the third person, the addressee of a joke] participate in the *Schaulust* [the desire to see], and to what extent is he exposed to, or by, the joke? And what if this "he" were a "she"?' (p. 111). This allows me to suggest that both Wollstonecraft's Vindications may be read, if not as 'participating' in Burke's particular *Schaulust*, at least as being significantly shaped as indignant responses to the way *Reflections* exploits and instantiates customary assumptions about gender in the passages we are reading. In *Rights of Men*, Wollstonecraft contends with and attempts to overturn Burke's narrative precisely through a rhetoric of stripping away the oppressive customs and costumes through which the old order is thought to imprison its subjects (particularly women). As a 'third person feminine', Wollstonecraft deflates Burke's irony by making it literal, agreeing with it, and turning it back upon its teller: 'On this scheme of things', she quotes, noting Burke's irony but adding her own emphasis, 'a king *is* but a man; a queen *is* but a woman; a woman *is* but an animal, and an animal not of the highest order'. However, for Wollstonecraft, women's animality is not anatomical but cultural: this is 'All true, Sir', she counters, 'if she is not more attentive to the duties of humanity than queens and fashionable ladies in general are' (p. 54). Whereas for Burke, women need customs and costumes to conceal their animality, for Wollstonecraft fashionable manners, by displacing morals, reduce women to animals. The joke thus rebounds back on Burke and his politics (the teller is exposed by his own aesthetics): 'fashionable ladies' – ladies constituted through fashion and emblematic of Burke's 'beautiful' ideology – are indeed, she suggests, animals 'not of the highest order'. Thus, although Wollstonecraft's reading recognises the 'nonsense' of Burke's rhetoric, it takes seriously its historical moment and political ramifications.

VI

The implications of the queen's 'fall' are most powerfully realised by juxtaposing it with the other references to women which cluster around the description of 5–6 October. We have seen that two very different ranks of women are given roles in this scene – the 'celestial' queen of France and a mob of women variously represented as the squaws of 'American savages' (p. 159), 'women lost to shame' (p. 161) and 'the furies of hell' (p. 165). If the chivalric code necessarily refers only to the *ladies* it constitutes, it is thus based on the *exclusion* of those women who, through reasons of class, race, manners or appearance, do not fit the code. There is no place in Burke's aesthetics and politics for the disturbingly 'masculine' women who led the queen and king in 'triumph' from Versailles. If, as Paulson suggests, these women 'in effect *are* the Revolution' (p. 81), they would seem to be the very antitype, politically and aesthetically, of Marie

Antoinette. Yet it might be that this exclusion depends upon the occlusion of that within the 'lady' which precisely relates her to those other women and so cuts across the differences in rank which Burke seeks to maintain.

This possibility can be explored by re-examining Burke's account of the Versailles incident in terms of the way it engages with contemporary textual productions of that event which stress instabilities of gender and dress. George Rudé's modern discussion of the episode shows that in the days leading up to the march to Versailles 'it was [the women] rather than the men that played the leading role in the movement': 'As they set out, in the early afternoon', he tells us, quoting a contemporary account, 'they . . . compelled every sort and condition of woman that they met – "même des femmes à chapeau" – to join them'.[18] The detail of dress is important because it signals that there were aristocratic women – or at least women dressed *like* aristocrats (prostitutes also dressed in high fashion) – taking part in the march. The revolutionary movement therefore involves, undecidably, either a real collusion between women of different classes or a transgression of the differences between them through the exploitation of sartorial conventions. *The Times* of 10 October 1789 reports that the women of Paris, under fear of famine, 'have even taken up arms, some with bludgeons, some with firelocks, and are hourly joined by large numbers of their sex'. It further reports (on 12 October) that most of the crowd that marched to Versailles were 'chiefly Fisherwomen', while many of those who forced their way into the palace were guards 'habited in women's dresses'. Although Natalie Z. Davis writes that such a disguise was 'surprisingly frequent' in riots and rebellions in seventeenth- and eighteenth-century France, her account of its advantages makes it seem not at all surprising, since it served the practical purpose of concealment, released men from full responsibility, and exploited 'the sexual power and energy of the unruly woman and . . . her license (which they had long assumed at carnival and games) . . . to tell the truth about unjust rule'.[19] Sekora discusses the political and cultural importance that has been accorded to sartorial conventions in hierarchical societies and points out their crucial roles in cities, where

the obvious badges of farm labor would be missing or cunningly disguised, and subversive persons – artisans, mechanics, servants, women, and young people – might congregate in numbers. Hence the gravity of laws defining status and costume in Athens and Rome and later in Genoa, Venice, Paris – and London.

(p. 56)

Later in his study, Sekora quotes from Samuel Fawconer's *Essay on Modern Luxury* of 1765:

> The custom of all civilised countries, hath regulated some general standard of dress, as most convenient to discriminate one from another in point of sex, age, and quality. The propriety and necessity of such a regulation, is evident from the mischiefs that could ensue from the want or neglect of it. For on whatever levelling principle the reasonable distinction of merit and degree is confounded, the order of government is broken in upon and destroyed.

(p. 100)

Burke is therefore eager to exclude these revolutionary 'women' from legitimate political activity precisely because their cross-dressing threatens to break in upon and destroy the order of government. This is brought out in his reference to those 'women lost to shame' who 'direct, control, applaud, [and] explode' the members of the National Assembly 'and sometimes mix and take their seats amongst them' (p. 161). These unrepresentable and unrepresented women shamelessly invade traditionally male territory and transgress the proper distinction between the people and their representative assembly. By not keeping to their place – any of the places assigned to them – they emblematically unsettle representative structures *per se*.

In *Reflections*, however, there are yet more subversions of differences in this intriguing moment. For Burke's text refers not simply to 'masculine' women, but to 'furies of hell, *in the abused shape* of the vilest of women' (my emphasis). It is not simply that men may have *assumed* the garb of women, or even that women have taken on the attributes of men, but that it is no longer possible to tell the difference – no longer possible to assign a fixed gender to either of the revolutionary sexes. These fiendish beings might be women with an 'abused' shape brought on by 'unfeminine' labour or 'masculine' behaviour, but they might equally be men making use of – and thus 'abusing' – women's 'shape' for disguise. There is no telling what one would find if these 'furies from hell' were stripped of their garb – an anxiety perhaps registered in Burke's emphasis on their 'infamous contumelies' (not only their insulting language, but their insolent swellings or tumescence). What seems to disturb Burke is not only that these 'women' do not adopt the pleasing illusions that aristocratic women clothe and paint themselves with, but that the garb they do wear and their behavioural habits and mannerisms have neither a 'natural' nor a traditional relation to their sex. The revolutionary mob thus disrupts the neat hierarchy between men and women *and* the stability of social signs in one and the same moment.

Burke, of course, makes great efforts to distinguish Marie Antoinette – his embodiment of aristocratic ideology, aesthetics, and womanhood – from what even Wollstonecraft calls 'the lowest refuse of the streets, women who had thrown off the virtues of one sex without having power to assume more than the vices of the other'.[20] But we have seen that when she is stripped of the clothes that seem simply to mark her distinction – when bereft of all 'the decent drapery of life' – the queen turns out to be 'but a woman', and therefore, in Burke's book, 'an animal not of the highest order'. In some uncanny way, then, she turns out to be horrifyingly *akin* to those yelling, screaming furies in the shape of 'the vilest of women' (p. 165) – as well as to those 'women lost to shame' who domineer over the National Assembly (p. 161), and to those American Indian women 'as ferocious' as their 'savage' men 'after some of their murders called victories' (p. 159). The social and cultural distinctions crucial to the maintenance of political order – those between classes and those between savagery and the epitome of civilisation – are suddenly and terrifyingly undercut in the revolutionary moment. Not only is the natural motivation of social signs shown to be disturbingly arbitrary at the lower end of the scale, but so too is that of the sign *par excellence* of aristocratic and monarchic order: the difference between the queen and the 'vilest of women' turns out to be merely a matter of dress and manners. But it is important to reiterate the fact that Burke's text does not stand outside this process and simply watch or record it in horror, since it is *Reflections* which itself brings together those kinds of women it endeavours to distinguish;[21] as the agent of those violations (of women, of class and gender distinctions) it would have its readers recoil from, Burke's text emerges as uncannily revolutionary in its most reactionary moment.

The slippage of the conventional signs of gender and class which Burke's account of the Versailles incident sets in motion may be seen as the quintessential revolutionary paradigm for Burke because it unsettles what Ferguson reads as the unifying analogical ground of his aesthetics and politics. For if much of the *Enquiry* tries to account for aesthetic responses in terms of 'the *properties* of external objects', Ferguson writes, so political legitimacy is derived, in *Reflections*, 'from its basis in *property*':

> Property produces legitimate government for him, just as the properties of aesthetic objects command responses to their beauty or sublimity. The difficulty that appears with the French Revolution, however, is that the very possibility of a drastic change registers the unnaturalness of nature by laying bare the fact that the properties of things, as well as the property belonging to any particular group in power, do not necessarily compel assent.[22]

Given this, I would suggest that if women's 'properties' (their appearance, dress, manners) are found to bear no necessary relation to their 'true nature', then a dizzying chasm opens up at the centre of Burke's aesthetic ideology. That women's properties seem arbitrary might imply that men's property over them – and consequently the 'legitimacy' of their own titles and title deeds – can never be authentically grounded. And yet I would argue that this possibility is not antithetical to Burke's thought, as Ferguson implies, but already potential within it. For the *Enquiry* not only explores the aesthetic effects of natural objects but also of words – which 'affect us in a manner very different from that in which we are affected by natural objects' (*Enquiry*, p. 163). In Burke's theory of language, words have no essential or natural properties; their power derives entirely from conventional associations which become 'legitimate' through long usage.[23] This process has its political analogue in *Reflections*, where Burke establishes the right to property and the legitimacy of any form of government though the notion of 'prescription', which attempts to justify the ownership of property – no matter how it was attained – through longevity of possession.[24] In other words, despite his protestations to the contrary, Burke's texts suggest that political, linguistic and aesthetic power arise solely through convention and have no basis in natural properties or property. Thus, Marie Antoinette emerges, precisely, as a conventional *sign* of traditional authority, the instabilities of which are not accidental but intrinsic to Burke's political and aesthetic system. The disturbing thing about her fall is that it exposes for all to see the principle that political power is grounded not in landed property itself, but in a set of conventional codes whose force depends solely on the fact that they *are* conventional. This problem is compounded in a historical moment in which political power is in the process of shifting from an economic basis in agrarian production to a more modern capitalist system in which the arbitrary status of wealth is not only more prominent but intrinsic to its system (in that it is based on mobile capital rather than in land). For Burke, this is a 'defect' which needs to be concealed if the people are to continue to regard the signs and codes of political power as natural.

VII

One of the remarkable things about Wollstonecraft's critique of the interplay between aesthetics, gender and politics in Burke's *Reflections* is not simply that she draws on Burke's *Enquiry* in order to point out his 'inconsistencies', but that she finds in the *Enquiry* a powerful articulation of her own political philosophy. Her two Vindications take on the basic assumptions of the *Enquiry* (about the virtues of 'manly' exertion and the dangers of 'feminine' luxury) and employ them for a feminist bourgeois project by identifying the feminine with the *ancien régime* and the masculine with revolutionary thought and activity. She thus challenges conventional assumptions about the relation between gender characteristics and sexual anatomy by insisting that the 'manly' and the 'feminine' are, at best, unnatural exaggerations of physiological differences between the sexes. This challenge is announced, with ironic humour, in the 'Author's Introduction' to *Rights of Woman* (1792):

> I am aware of an obvious inference. From every quarter have I heard exclamations against masculine women, but where are they to be found? If by this appellation men mean to inveigh against their ardour in hunting, shooting, and gaming, I shall most cordially join in the cry; but if it be against the imitation of manly virtues, or, more properly speaking, the attainment of those talents and virtues, the exercise of which ennobles the human character, and which raises females in the scale of animal being, . . . all those who view them with a philosophic eye must . . . wish with

me, that they may every day grow more and more masculine.[25]

Sharing the way the *Enquiry* values the masculine over the
feminine, Wollstonecraft strives to make 'manly virtues' available
to women as an antidote to the debilitating feminisation forced
upon them by aristocratic patriarchy. In this way, she is also able
to reveal that one of the internal contradictions of *Reflections* is
that its defence of the *ancien régime* runs counter to some of the
fundamental insights of the *Enquiry*. She thus forces us to
speculate on the implications of the fact that her revolutionary
politics often seem more consistent with Burke's *Enquiry* than are
the politics of Burke's own *Reflections*.

For Wollstonecraft, both kinds of women brought into violent
confrontation in Burke's narrative are symptomatic products of
the *ancien régime*: aristocratic woman embodies the deceptive
ideology and aesthetics of the old order (in which women are
both loved and despised because of their precarious and dangerous beauty), while 'the lowest refuse of the streets' represent her
inverse image. In *Rights of Men*, Wollstonecraft claims that the
aristocratic social formation necessarily produces the 'vulgar' – a
term which

> not only . . . describe[s] a class of people, who, working to
> support the body, have not had time to cultivate their minds;
> but likewise those who, born in the lap of affluence, have
> never had their invention sharpened by necessity [and who]
> are, nine out of ten, the creatures of habit and impulse.
>
> (p. 28)

The lower classes and the aristocracy are thus made significantly
analogous in that, although the former labour incessantly while
the latter luxuriate, the faculties of both atrophy through lack of
exercise. Neither class enjoys – in an image which comes to be a
watchword of Wollstonecraft's texts – a 'manly spirit of independence' (*Rights of Men*, p. 28). This lends support to Paulson's
suggestion that the beautiful and the brutal represent 'the two
aspects of women which she saw as the heart of the problem
raised by the French Revolution' (p. 84). Both types of women are
potentially recoverable, in Wollstonecraft's theory, through the
revolutionary process. If one needs to be stripped of veils of
illusion that foster and disguise vices degrading to humanity (and
hence be transformed from a debilitating into an invigorating
emblem of the beautiful), the other might be educated from an

undisciplined grotesque into a sublime force.[26] Thus, Wollstonecraft reacts to Burke's portrait of the women who marched
to Versailles by attempting to substitute an 'historical' account for
his 'hysterical' rhetoric:

> Probably you mean women who gained a livelihood by
> selling vegetables or fish, who never had any advantages of
> education; or their vices might have lost part of their
> abominable deformity, by losing part of their grossness.
>
> (*Rights of Men*, pp. 67–68)

In this way, Wollstonecraft gives an ironic twist to Burke's lament
that 'the age of chivalry is gone', and along with it the 'unbought
grace of life . . . under which vice lost half its evil, by losing all its
grossness' (*Reflections*, p. 170). And yet despite such witty
recognitions that the characteristics of upper and lower class
women are products of a particular social formation, Wollstonecraft remains disconcerted by them. In *Rights of Woman*, she
admits that she is primarily concerned to address women 'in the
middle class, because they appear to be in the most natural state'
(p. 81).

If, as Ferguson suggests, 'all [the sublime's] strivings [in the
Enquiry] follow the dictates of the work ethic' ('Sublime of
Edmund Burke', p. 76), then it seems appropriate less to heroic
than to bourgeois enterprise. Thus when Paulson alerts us to the
fact that Wollstonecraft's 'favorite terms are *exercise* and *exert*'
(p. 85), we can begin to see how she conflates her feminist and
bourgeois interests through attacking Burke on (and in) his own
terms. By wishing to replace what she describes as a 'beauty
[which] relaxes the solids of the soul as well as the body' with a
virtuous beauty 'which necessarily implies exertion' (*Rights of
Men*, pp. 115–16), Wollstonecraft both uses Burke's *Enquiry* to
criticise his later defence of an enervated and enervating political
system and 'defeminises' his notion of the beautiful in order to
make it a virtuous aesthetic equally attainable by men and
women. This is why Wollstonecraft, from the opening pages of
her critique, rewrites both of Burke's aesthetic categories for a
new ethics and ideology: 'truth, in morals, has ever appeared to
me the essence of the sublime; and, in taste, simplicity the only
criterion of the beautiful' (*Rights of Men*, p. 2).[27] Conversely, this
enables her to feminise Burke by ironically pointing out the
'defects' of his 'theatrical attitudes' and 'sentimental exclamations' which 'cover a multitude of vices' (p. 5). Addressing

Burke directly, Wollstonecraft claims to 'shew you to yourself, stripped of the gorgeous drapery in which you have enwrapped your tyrannic principles' (p. 88).

Wollstonecraft identifies Burke's pleasing illusions, which blind citizens to a country's defects, as 'gothic notions of beauty' – an 'ivy' which, although it might be 'beautiful', parasitically undermines what it adorns: 'when it insidiously destroys the trunk from which it receives support, who would not grub it up?' (*Rights of Men*, p. 10). Drawing on Burke's *Enquiry*, Wollstonecraft suggests that the system of manners and habitual, unthinking affections towards traditional institutions which Burke recommends in *Reflections* are the very things which are most dangerous to human and political constitutions: truth should be demonstrated by reason 'and not determined by arbitrary authority and dark traditions, lest a dangerous supineness should take place' (p. 37). It is not blind habit which raises us above the brutes, but the exercise of reason, which can only be acquired through exertion (pp. 70–71, 77).[28] In fact, the debilitating effects of the system Burke apparently wishes to perpetuate are already to be seen in 'the noble families which form one of the pillars of our state' (pp. 51–52), in the sexual behaviour of husbands and wives (pp. 52–53) and in the language of contemporary discourse (pp. 64–66). Under the system of arranged marriages and primogeniture through which aristocratic families perpetuate their name, for example, 'Our young men become selfish coxcombs, and gallantry with modest women, and intrigues with those of another description, weaken both mind and body, before either has arrived at maturity' (*Rights of Men*, p. 47). Rather than encouraging men to adopt their 'proper' roles as husbands and fathers – roles which produce 'a sober manliness of thought' – such a system produces 'finical [men] of taste' (p. 47) and 'young men of fashion' (p. 92). This artificial system 'has an equally pernicious effect on female morals', producing 'women of fashion [who] take husbands that they may have it in their power to coquet, the grand business of genteel life . . . without . . . being of any use to society' (pp. 47–48). Such 'women of fashion' are not, then, following the dictates of their 'feminine' nature, but are, like their male counterparts, *fashioned* by this artificial system. In a meritocracy, by contrast, 'Luxury and effeminacy would not . . . introduce so much idiotism into the noble families which form one of the pillars of our state' (p. 51). In such conditions, 'Women would probably then act like mothers, and the fine lady, become a rational woman' (p. 52).

On the basis of these passages it may be observed that Wollstonecraft does not simply repeat Burke's elevation of the sublime and consequent degradation of the beautiful. Paulson claims that 'The underlying insight of Wollstonecraft's writings on the French Revolution is that the beautiful is no longer a viable aesthetic category' (p. 86), and this might appear a perfectly valid reading – after all, Wollstonecraft does say that 'if we really wish to render men more virtuous, we must endeavour to banish all enervating modifications of beauty from civil society' (*Rights of Men*, p. 115). But Paulson's conclusion can only be sustained through partial quotation. Wollstonecraft would grub up the 'gothic' ivy of the *ancien régime* because its destructive effects are most characteristically displayed in the systematic enervation of women. This cosmetic beauty is the informing aesthetic of that 'Gothic gallantry' (p. 89) which 'vitiates' women and 'prevents their endeavouring to obtain solid personal merit . . . [and makes them] vain inconsiderate dolls' (p. 54). But Wollstonecraft does more than expose the aesthetic and ideological implications of this beauty in order symbolically to strip Marie Antoinette for different ends than Burke. We have seen that she also offers an alternative understanding of beauty – one which is based on the classical and neo-classical models which Burke's treatise rejects but which transforms them for an egalitarian politics whose very ground is the equality of the sexes and the reconciliation of the sublime and the beautiful:

> But should experience prove that there is a beauty in virtue, a charm in order, which necessarily implies exertion, a depraved sensual taste may give way to a more manly one – and *melting* feelings to rational satisfactions. Both may be equally natural to man; the test is their moral difference, and that point reason alone can decide.
>
> (*Rights of Men*, p. 116)

This is a breathtaking passage because it momentarily shifts the debate from what is 'natural' by suggesting that both kinds of aesthetic or society may be equally based on human nature, and that the only testing ground for a political system and its attendant aesthetic is therefore to 'reason' upon its 'moral' – that is individual and social – consequences.

'Such a glorious change', she continues, 'can only be produced by liberty. Inequality of rank must ever impede the growth of virtue, by vitiating the mind that submits or domineers' (p. 116). Thus, her politics and ethics admit of neither submission nor dominance, neither lordship nor servitude; they can only flourish in a society based on equality in gender and class. If 'society' in Burke's *Enquiry* is implicitly feminised and disparaged in comparison to the 'manly' solitude of sublimity, 'society' in Wollstonecraft is only possible where hierarchies of class and gender have been levelled: 'Among unequals there can be no society; – giving a manly meaning to the term' (p. 92). It follows from this that radicalism's project to achieve equality between men cannot succeed unless the inequality between men and women which underlies the old order is also confronted. Wollstonecraft thus shows that the two forms of inequality are inextricably symptomatic of each other and that political reform necessarily implies reform in those aesthetics, manners and rhetorical practices which contribute towards the inequality between men and women as well as between classes. She therefore looks to the French revolutionaries to see if they 'can produce a crisis' which will usher in the change. Only in the National Assembly is government guided by 'unsophisticated reason' and promoted by 'exertions that [are] not relaxed by a fastidious respect for the beauty of rank' (p. 117).

In *Rights of Woman* two years later, Wollstonecraft directs her critique principally against Rousseau's negative account of women in *Emile.* This had become strategically necessary – given the importance of Rousseau for revolutionary thought – since the National Assembly was in the process of producing a constitution which excluded women from participating in the 'rights of men'. Failing to live up to the expectations Wollstonecraft had for it in *Rights of Men,* the Revolution was therefore developing in a way which would undermine itself from within:

> if women are to be excluded, without having a voice, from a participation of the natural rights of mankind, prove first, to ward off the charge of injustice and inconsistency, that they want reason, else this flaw in your NEW CONSTITUTION will ever show that man must, in some shape, act like a tyrant, and tyranny, in whatever part of society it rears its brazen front, will ever undermine morality.
>
> (*Rights of Woman,* p. 88)

In an intriguing twist, then, Wollstonecraft uses the insights gained from her reading of Burke in an attempt to intervene in the

National Assembly's deliberations. We have seen that Burke's *Enquiry* constitutes the sublime as an antidote to the debilitating effects of the beautiful through the bracing effects of labour, and that *Reflections* laments the fact that the events of 5–6 October have initiated a 'revolution in sentiments, manners and moral opinions' (*Reflections*, p. 175). Wollstonecraft appropriates the earlier configuration and turns it against the later one in order to stress to her radical readers that 'It is time to effect a revolution in female manners . . . and make them, as a part of the human species, labour by reforming themselves to reform the world' (*Rights of Woman*, p. 132).

But although she thus identifies the complex interrelation between Burke's early aesthetics and late politics, Wollstonecraft's use of the former to point out the contradictions of the latter means that she ends up endorsing Burke's negative evaluation of the feminine in the very process of placing women in the vanguard of revolutionary action.[29] Her revolution in female subjectivity is thereby defined against and continually threatened by that which it excludes as 'other' (the 'animality' of 'vain inconsiderate dolls' on the one hand and of 'the lowest refuse of the streets' on the other).[30] The symptoms of such a self-undermining relation to the feminine 'other' are most readily seen by setting Wollstonecraft's treatment of Marie Antoinette alongside Burke's. In her *Historical and Moral View of the Origin and Progress of the French Revolution* of 1794, Wollstonecraft presents Marie Antoinette as a 'young and beautiful *dauphine*' arriving at a French Court whose 'general depravation of manners' would inevitably corrupt her character: 'In such a voluptuous atmosphere, how could she escape contagion?' (p. 33). Developing into a woman 'with all those complacent graces which dance round flattered beauty, whose every charm is drawn forth by the consciousness of pleasing' (p. 131), Marie Antoinette is made to embody everything which *Rights of Woman* was written to contest. Given the basic principles of her two Vindications, however, it might be thought that Wollstonecraft would have condoned the queen's efforts to cast off the constraints of courtly etiquette in France in favour of a more 'natural' style of dress and behaviour. The Burkean terms she uses to criticise Marie Antoinette therefore indicate how important it is for Wollstonecraft to condemn her:

> Constrained by the *etiquette*, which made the principle part of the imposing grandeur of Louis XIV, the queen wished to

throw aside the cumbersome brocade of ceremony, without having discernment enough to perceive, that it was necessary to lend mock dignity to a court, where there was not sufficient virtue, or native beauty, to give interest or respectability to simplicity. The harlot is seldom such a fool as to neglect her meretricious ornaments, unless she renounces her trade; and the pageantry of courts is the same thing on a larger scale.

(Historical and Moral View, pp. 34–35)

Rather than receiving praise for anticipating or enabling the Revolution, Marie Antoinette is figured as a harlot who, not knowing the conditions of her own trade, divests herself and the French court of their 'meretricious ornaments'. Unexpectedly echoing Burke's lamentation over the Revolution's violation of the 'pleasing illusions' of the *ancien régime*, Wollstonecraft suggests that the queen was guilty of 'destroying all reverence for . . . majesty' in France by stripping it 'of the frippery which had concealed it's deformity' (p. 35). By thus employing the terms with which Burke describes the queen's treatment at the hands of the revolutionary mob, Wollstonecraft seems to suggest that the brutalities of the Revolution originate in Marie Antoinette's lack of 'discernment'. Although she condemns the events at Versailles even more vehemently than Burke (referring to the perpetrators as 'a set of monsters, distinct from the people' [p. 450]), Wollstonecraft's unease with Marie Antoinette (derived from her reading of Burke's aesthetics) thus leads her to imply that she deserved the fate which Burke scripts for her in *Reflections*.

References

1. Kaplan, Cora (1985). 'Pandora's box: subjectivity, class and sexuality in socialist feminist criticism', in Gayle Greene and Coppélia Kahn (eds.) *Making a Difference: Feminist Literary Criticism*. London, Methuen, pp. 146–76 (164).
2. All quotations from Burke's *Reflections* are taken from Burke, Edmund (1790). *Reflections on the Revolution in France*. Conor Cruise O'Brien (ed.) (1968) Harmondsworth, Penguin. For the claim that Burke's representation of the events of 5–6 October 1789 is the 'centrepiece of the *Reflections*', see Boulton, James T. (1963). *The Language of Politics in the Age of Wilkes and Burke*. London, Routledge & Kegan Paul, pp. 98 and 127–33.
3. All quotations from Wollstonecraft's *Rights of Men* are taken from Wollstonecraft, Mary (1790). *A Vindication of the Rights of Men*.

Eleanor Louise Nicholes (intr.) (1960). Gainesville, Florida, Scholars' Facsimiles & Reprints. All quotations from Burke's *Enquiry* are taken from Burke, Edmund (1757/59). *A Philosophical Enquiry into the Origin of Our Ideas of the Sublime and Beautiful*. James T. Boulton (ed.) (1958). London, Routledge & Kegan Paul.

4. See Sekora, John (1977). *Luxury: The Concept in Western Thought, Eden to Smollett*. Baltimore and London, The Johns Hopkins University Press, pp. 63–131. For a more extended discussion of the political implications of the way Burke's *Enquiry* responds to the notion of luxury, see Furniss, Tom (1991). 'Edmund Burke: Bourgeois Revolutionary in a Radical Crisis', in Peter Osborne (ed.) *Socialism and the Limits of Liberalism*. London, Verso, pp. 15–50.

5. Ferguson, Frances (1981). 'The Sublime of Edmund Burke, Or the Bathos of Experience', *Glyph: Johns Hopkins Textual Studies*, 8, 62–78 (69).

6. Cobban, Alfred (1957, 1963). *A History of Modern France: Volume 1: 1715–1799*. Harmondsworth, Penguin, pp. 161–62.

7. Price, Richard (1789). *A Discourse on the Love of Our Country*. London, Cadell, p. 49.

8. For a discussion which examines the way Burke's use of theatrical metaphors throughout his representation of the events of 5–6 October 1789 actually dramatises the internal contradictions which drive his text, see Furniss, Tom. 'Stripping the Queen: Edmund Burke's Magic Lantern Show', in Steven Blakemore (ed.) *Burke and the French Revolution: Bicentenary Studies*. Athens, Georgia, The University of Georgia Press, forthcoming.

9. See Macpherson, C.B. (1980). *Burke*. Oxford, Oxford University Press, pp. 1–7, and 51–70.

10. One should be wary of reading such passages as unequivocal attempts on Burke' part to 'feminise' society. Echoes of the *Enquiry* among these passages suggest that they are driven by contradictory impulses. At the end of passages which seem to encourage the softening of monarchical authority, for example, Burke obliquely suggests that Louis XVI's only fault was not to have been stern enough:

> I shall never think that a prince, the acts of whose whole reign were a series of concessions to his subjects, who was willing to relax his authority . . . to call his people to a share of freedom, not known, perhaps not desired by their ancestors . . . deserves the cruel and insulting triumph of Paris, and of Dr Price. I tremble for the cause of liberty, from such an example to kings. . . . But there are some people of that low and degenerate fashion of mind, that they look up with a sort of complacent awe and admiration to kings, who know to keep firm in their seat, to hold a strict hand over their subjects . . . and by the awakened

vigilance of a severe despotism, to guard against the very first approaches of freedom.

(*Reflections*, pp. 177–78)

This is an ambiguous passage in that it seems impossible to draw from it the exact attitude Burke is recommending towards reform. The first sentence suggests a sympathy with Louis XVI and his enlightened measures, and yet there is the implication that the people who could treat such a liberal monarch as they did on 5–6 October are not fit for freedoms 'perhaps not desired by their ancestors'. The third sentence compounds this ambiguity, in that although it seems to condemn 'severe despotism', it is especially contemptuous of those who, looking up to it with 'complacent awe and admiration', seem to deserve their own subjugation. And in terms of Burke's aesthetics, what appears at first sight to be a preference for liberal reform over despotism can be read in an exactly opposite way – for in the *Enquiry*, as we have seen, Burke strenuously urges an 'awakened vigilance' against the dangers of relaxation. Thus this passage can read as both a lament for and criticism of Louis XVI – and in turn as an object lesson for those members of Britain's ruling classes currently seeking liberal reform.

11. Rousseau, Jean-Jacques (1781, posthumous). *The Confessions*. J.M. Cohen (tr.) (1953). Harmondsworth, Penguin, p. 362; Rousseau is referring to his *Discourse on the Origin of Inequality* (1755).

12. Paulson, Ronald (1983). *Representations of Revolution (1789–1820)*. New Haven and London, Yale University Press, pp. 62, 65, 61. Paulson's analysis of this passage draws on Isaac Kramnick (1977). *The Rage of Edmund Burke: Portrait of an Ambivalent Conservative*. New York, Basic Books, pp. 151–57.

13. The exposure of women becomes a paradigmatic moment of revolution in France, mobilising equivocal political, psychic and sexual connotations. Describing the 'June Days' of 1848, Victor Hugo writes that, at a certain crucial moment, with the National Guard advancing,

> a woman appeared on the crest of the first barricade, a young woman, beautiful, dishevelled, terrifying. This woman, who was a public whore, pulled her dress up to her waist and cried out to the guardsmen, in that dreadful brothel language that one is always obliged to translate: 'Cowards! Fire, if you dare, at the belly of a woman!' Here things took an awful turn. The National Guard did not hesitate. A fusillade toppled the miserable creature. She fell with a great cry. There was a horrified silence at the barricade and among the attackers.
>
> (Victor Hugo, 'Chose vues', *Oeuvres completes*, 35 vols. Paris, Martell, 1955, vol. 31, pp. 365–66, quoted [and presumably translated] by Neil Hertz [1985]. 'Medusa's Head: Male Hysteria

under Political Pressure'. *The End of the Line: Essays on Psycho-analysis and the Sublime*. New York, Columbia University Press, pp. 160–215 [163])

'The June uprising', Hugo writes, immediately before this passage, 'right from the start, presented strange lineaments. It displayed suddenly, to a horrified society, monstrous and unknown forms'. From this, Hertz argues that 'what the revolution is said to be doing figuratively is precisely what – in a moment – . . . the [woman] will be represented as doing literally' (p. 164). Hertz reads this passage in psychoanalytical terms, suggesting that it invokes the male anxiety of castration, but for an alternative – more 'historical' – reading see Catherine Gallagher's 'Response' (*End of the Line*, pp. 194–96).

14. For Freud's account of what he calls the *'obscene* joke', see Freud, Sigmund (1905). *Jokes and their Relation to the Unconscious*. James Strachey (tr.) and Angela Richards (ed.) (1960, 1976). Harmonds-worth, Penguin, pp. 140–45.

15. Weber, Samuel (1982). *The Legend of Freud*. Minneapolis, University of Minnesota Press, pp. 102, 104.

16. For Freud's discussion of the relation between jokes and social conventions, see *Jokes*, pp. 191–211.

17. For a discussion of the political and literary features of the carnival, see Bakhtin, Mikhail (1984). *Problems of Dostoevsky's Poetics*. Caryl Emerson (tr.) Manchester, Manchester University Press, pp. 122–37.

18. Rudé, George (1959, 1967). *The Crowd in the French Revolution*. Oxford, Oxford University Press, pp. 69, 75.

19. Davis, Natalie Z. (1975). *Society and Culture in Early Modern France*. California, Stanford, pp. 147–50.

20. Wollstonecraft, Mary (1794/95). *An Historical and Moral View of the Origin and Progress of the French Revolution: and the Effect It Has Produced in Europe*. Janet Todd (intr.) (1975). Facsimile reproduction of second edition, Delmar, Scholars' Facsimiles and Reprints, p. 426. (For Wollstonecraft's full account of the events of 5–6 October, see pp. 420–69.) That the virtues and vices characteristic of each gender and class may be thrown off or assumed in this way suggests that they function more like clothes than natural properties.

21. Craig Howes discusses Burke's account of 5–6 October specifically as an attempt to dissociate elements which it (paradoxically) brings together:

> the bedchamber scene from the *Reflections* . . . sharply contrasts the mob's Satanic, violating power with the helpless, half-dressed, fleeing figure of the beautiful Marie Antoinette. When power does erupt in women, as in the march to Versailles, they become possessed harpies, desexed and foul.
> (Howes, Craig [1985]. 'Burke, Poe, and "Usher": The Sublime

and Rising Woman', *ESQ: A Journal of the American Renaissance*, 31, iii, pp. 173–89 [184])

22. Ferguson, Frances (1985). 'Legislating the Sublime', in Ralph Cohen (ed.) *Studies in Eighteenth-Century British Art and Aesthetics*. California, University of California Press, pp. 128–47 (137–38).
23. In the *Enquiry*, words such as 'virtue, liberty, or honour' 'are in reality but mere sounds; but they are sounds, which being used on particular occasions . . . they produce in the mind, whenever they are afterwards mentioned, effects similar to those of their occasions' (p. 165).
24. Burke attacks the Revolution not because of its violent usurpation of power but because such usurpation may not have been absolutely necessary:

> If they had set up this new experimental government as a necessary substitute for an expelled tyranny, mankind would anticipate the time of prescription, which, through long usage, mellows into legality governments that were violent in their commencement.
>
> (*Reflections*, p. 276).

For a discussion of the way Burke uses the notion of prescription to show how the usurpation of landed property in the past 'mellows' into legal ownership, see Lucas, Paul (1968). 'On Edmund Burke's Doctrine of Prescription; Or an Appeal from the New to the Old Lawyers', *The Historical Journal*, xi, 35–63.
25. Wollstonecraft, Mary (1792). *Vindication of the Rights of Woman*. Miriam Brody Kramnick (ed.) Harmondsworth, Penguin, p. 80.
26. This point is derived from Paulson, *Representations of Revolution*, pp. 86–87.
27. Wollstonecraft implicitly engages with and attempts to revise Burke's influential formulations of the sublime and the beautiful throughout *Rights of Men*, but her critique becomes explicit at one crucial point. Alluding to rumours that 'fair ladies' in America not only concur with the ill treatment of negro slaves but 'invent' additional 'unheard of tortures' for them, she suggests that 'after the sight of a flagellation' these ladies probably 'compose their ruffled spirits and exercise their tender feelings by the perusal of the last imported novel' (p. 111). Such women, who could shed 'tears' in response to fictional sentiment while being coldly indifferent to actual suffering, are said to typify the inevitable results of Burke's aesthetics:

> But these ladies may have read your Enquiry concerning the origin of our ideas of the Sublime and Beautiful, and, convinced by your arguments, may have laboured to be pretty, by counterfeiting weakness.

> You may have convinced them that *littleness* and *weakness* are the very essence of beauty; and that the Supreme Being, in giving women beauty in the most supereminent degree, seemed to command them, by the powerful voice of Nature, not to cultivate the moral virtues that might chance to excite respect, and interfere with the pleasing sensations they were created to inspire. Thus confining truth, fortitude, and humanity, within the rigid pale of manly morals, they might justly argue, that to be loved, women's high end and great distinction! they should 'learn to lisp, to totter in their walk, and nick-name God's creatures'
>
> (pp. 111–12).

Fusing an allusion to *Hamlet* (3.1.147–49) with an allusion to Burke's *Enquiry* (p. 110), Wollstonecraft identifies the effects of the Burkean concept of women precisely as inducing impediments of mobility and speech. Under such social mores, Wollstonecraft notes ironically, women *labour* in order to create the impression of being incapable of labour.

28. Wollstonecraft's analysis leads her to reverse Burke's assessment of manners: 'like every custom that an arbitrary point of honour has established, [the civilisation of Europe] refines the manners at the expence of morals' (*Rights of Men*, p. 11). At the same time, in a revealing comment, 'the cultivation of reason is an arduous task . . . happy is it for [the indolent] . . . that some virtuous habits, with which the reason of others shackled them, supplies its place' (p. 71). This is curiously to repeat Burke's formula, and suggests that the tangles of Burke's texts are not peculiar to them but endemic to the terms in which eighteenth-century discourse conceived and confronted its political and aesthetic problems.

29. Kaplan sketches a similar relation between Wollstonecraft and Rousseau: 'By defending women against Rousseau's denial of their reason, Wollstonecraft unwittingly assents to his negative, eroticised sketch of their emotional lives' ('Subjectivity, class and sexuality', p. 158).

30. Kaplan claims that 'The new categories of independent subjectivity [produced in late eighteenth-century republican discourse on both sides of the Atlantic] were marked from the beginning by exclusions of gender, race and class' ('Subjectivity, class, and sexuality', p. 150). Even though she argues that such discourses 'shaped, and were shaped by, the ways in which women of the middle and upper classes understood and represented their own being', and even though she claims that such women were thereby 'led . . . towards projecting and displacing on to women of lower social standing and women of colour, as well as on to the "traditionally" corrupt aristocracy, all that was deemed vicious and regressive in women as

a sex', Kaplan finds it 'deeply troubling to find these projected and displaced representations in the writing of sexual and social radicals, and in the work of feminists from Wollstonecraft to Woolf, as well as in conservative sexual and social discourses' (p. 167).

5

'The cool eye of observation': Mary Wollstonecraft and the French Revolution

Harriet Devine Jump

In December 1794, Joseph Johnson published Mary Wollstonecraft's *An Historical and Moral View of the Origin and Progress of the French Revolution; and the Effect it has Produced in Europe. Volume the First.*[1] The *Historical and Moral View* is the longest of Wollstonecraft's works, and the least well-known today. According to her biographer Ralph M. Wardle, the work is 'devoid of autobiographical interest',[2] and since the 1790s it has received little critical attention. When it first appeared, however, it was greeted in the literary magazines with warmth and enthusiasm. Partly this was attributable to the fact that most of the reviewers apparently shared Wollstonecraft's political views. In addition, she was still enjoying the celebrity which had followed the favourable critical reception of her previous work, *A Vindication of the Rights of Woman*.[3] The *Critical Review* praised Wollstonecraft's 'strong mind', the 'high tone of her sentiments', her 'many just remarks and forcible observations'.[4] The *Analytical Review* called the work 'a production of genius', displaying 'energy of diction, and . . . richness of imagery . . . with a solidity and depth of thought which . . . we will venture to call truly philosophical';[5] the *Monthly Review* wrote that

> A mind naturally vigorous, inured to reflection, free from vulgar prejudices, and, as appears from her former works, accustomed to comprehensive views of nature and society,

Neil Evans

has qualified her to speculate on these facts judiciously and profoundly; and a lively and prolific imagination has enabled her to clothe her speculations with the grace of eloquence.[6]

Among all this praise, a single dissenting voice was heard; that of the British Critic, a publication which had been set up in 1793 by two Tory churchmen, Robert Nares and William Below, in deliberate opposition to the liberal dissenting opinions of the Critical, Analytical and Monthly Reviews.[7] This review could scarcely have been less favourable. It began by pointing out at some length the numerous borrowings which Wollstonecraft had made from the New Annual Register (the Register's own reviewer had failed to notice these, incidentally). The British Critic disapproved of Wollstonecraft's morality, took exception to her politics, and accused her of 'tinsel and tawdriness' of style.[8] Moreover, he found a fundamental flaw in Wollstonecraft's arguments:

> Sometimes she reasons solely upon what she calls first principles; at other times her sentiments are exclusively formed, on what has passed under her observation: and the deductions from these two sources refuse all blending, or union with each other.

(35)

A careful reading of the Historical and Moral View will reveal that amid the general disparagement, the reviewer has singled out a problem which lies at the heart of the work. For the twentieth-century reader, however, far from detracting from the book's interest, this in fact increases it. First, however, the circumstances of its composition and publication need to be placed in context.

The exact date on which Wollstonecraft began work on the Historical and Moral View is not known, but it must have been before 13 June 1793, when she wrote to her sister from Neuilly-sur-Seine that she was 'writing a great book'.[9] Although a number of factors had contributed to her decision to move to France at the end of the previous year,[10] as a professional writer she certainly felt an obligation to respond to the public demand for commentaries on the Revolution written by English sympathisers in situ.[11] She appears to have made an agreement to send a series of 'Letters on the Present Character of the French Nation' for publication by Johnson; but although the 'Letter: Introductory' to these, dated 15 February 1793, has survived, it remained unpublished until after her death, when it was published by Godwin in his edition of the *Posthumous Works of the Author of 'A Vindication of the Rights of Woman'*,[12] owing, no doubt, to her dissatisfaction with its tone and content.

Godwin later attributed her failure to continue with this project to the fact that she had been temporarily depressed and lonely when she arrived in Paris. He contended that the 'gloominess of her mind communicated its own colour to the objects she saw' and 'tinged [her writing] with the saturnine temper which at that time pervaded her mind'.[13] However, the one surviving 'Letter' reveals a more profound disturbance of mind than can be dismissed as merely the result of a passing depression. Although, admittedly, Wollstonecraft had left England partly to recover from an unhappy personal situation, she had chosen Paris as her destination because of her ardent support for the principles of the Revolution, which had, at its inception, produced 'a conspicuous effect in the progress of [her] reflections' (Godwin 1798: 74) and which she had defended warmly in her 1790 *Vindication of the Rights of Men*. Almost as soon as she arrived, however, she found herself quite unexpectedly in tears at the sight of Louis XVI 'sitting, with more dignity than I expected from his character, in a hackney coach going to meet death'. Later the same day – 26 December 1792 – she wrote to Johnson:

> I have been alone since; and, though my mind is calm, I cannot dismiss the lively images that have filled my imagination all the day. – Nay, do not smile, but pity me; for, once or twice, lifting my eyes from the paper, I have seen eyes glare through a glass-door opposite my chair, and bloody hands shook at me. Not the distant sound of a footstep can I hear. . . . I want to see something alive; death in so many frightful shapes has taken hold of my fancy. – I am going to bed – and, for the first time in my life, I cannot put out the candle.

> (Wardle 1979: 227)

By the middle of February 1793, when her 'Letter: Introductory' was apparently written, she had been further saddened by 'the striking contrast of riches and poverty, elegance and slovenliness, urbanity and deceit, [which] everywhere caught [her] eye' and by her increasing conviction that 'the morals of the people will not be much improved by the change, or the government rendered less venal' (Wollstonecraft 1793: 40, 43).

She was unable to refrain from expressing the most profound philosophical doubts:

> Before I came to France, I cherished . . . an opinion, that strong virtues might exist with the polished manners produced by the progress of civilization; and I even anticipated an epoch, when, in the course of improvement, men would labour to become virtuous, without being goaded on by misery. But now, the perspective of the golden age, fading before the attentive eye of observation, almost eludes my sight; and, losing thus in part my theory of a more perfect state, start not, my friend, if I bring forward an opinion, which at first sight seems to be levelled against the existence of God! I am not become an Atheist, I assure you, by residing at Paris: yet I begin to fear that vice, or, if you will, evil, is the grand mobile of action, and that, when the passions are justly poized, we become harmless, and in the same proportion useless.
>
> (Wollstonecraft 1793: 44–45)

The importance of this failure of philosophical optimism for Wollstonecraft can hardly be overestimated; if it had continued, it would have required a complete reappraisal of all her most fundamental beliefs. Such a reappraisal was, to a greater or lesser extent, forced on many of her contemporaries before many more years had passed; but in 1793 she was unable fully to accept the consequences, and as a result her next attempt at composition shows her undergoing some curious mental convolutions in order, as the *British Critic* put it, to blend and unify her observations with her belief – now tenuously revived – in first principles. Despite Godwin's assertion that the *Historical and Moral View* was written 'with more sobriety and cheerfulness' than her earlier 'Letter: Introductory' (Godwin 1798: 106), it is clear that many doubts still remained in her mind about the final outcome of events.

It is worth noting, however, that, while the 'Letter: Introductory' shows Wollstonecraft's philosophical optimism at its lowest ebb, she appears never to have participated in the excesses of millenial enthusiasm of many of her contemporaries. Her previous published comments on the Revolution had been made two years earlier in her answer to Burke, *A Vindication of the Rights of Men* (1790). Conscious that Burke had poured scorn on the millenarian claims made by Richard Price, who had exclaimed,

> What an eventful period this is! I am thankful that I have lived to see it; and I could almost say, *Lord, now lettest thou thy servant depart in peace, for mine eyes have seen thy salvation* . . .
> *(Discourse on the Love of our Country* 1799, 2nd edn: 49)

Wollstonecraft appears deliberately to have kept her enthusiasm within bounds:

> I am not, Sir, aware of your sneers, hailing a millenium, though a state of greater purity of morals may not be a mere poetic fiction; nor did my fancy ever create a heaven on earth, since reason threw off her swaddling clothes. . . . If we mean to build our knowledge or happiness on a rational basis, we must learn to distinguish the *possible*, and not fight against the stream. And if we are careful to guard ourselves from imaginary sorrows and vain fears, we must also resign many enchanting illusions . . .
> (Wollstonecraft 1790, 2nd edn: 76, 140)

Only once in this work does she allow herself an imaginative glimpse of a more paradisal future:

> What salutary dews might not be shed to refresh this thirsty land, if men were more *enlightened!* . . . A garden more inviting than Eden would then meet the eye, and springs of joy murmur on every side.
> (Wollstonecraft 1790, 2nd edn: 147)

Her note of restraint in this work, although no doubt partly self-imposed in pursuit of her object of demonstrating rationality in opposition to Burke's emotional rhetoric, makes a marked contrast with the millenarianism of many of the other replies to Burke which were published at this period: Joseph Priestley, for example, saw the Revolution as the beginning of that 'reign of peace' which had been 'distinctly and repeatedly foretold in many prophecies, delivered more than two thousand years ago',[14] and Catherine Macaulay – a writer much admired by Wollstonecraft – drew Burke's attention to 'some passages in the Revelations [which] point to a time when the *iron* sceptre of *arbitrary* sway shall be broken; when *righteousness shall prevail* over the whole earth . . .'[15]

The evidence of both the comments which Wollstonecraft published on the Revolution indicates that she was unwilling to use such direct scriptural evidence to validate the effects of events in France. However, the 'first principles' to which she continually returns in the *Historical and Moral View* are clearly more moderate and secular expressions of the millenialist belief, common at this period, that both men and political systems were naturally moving towards a more perfect state.[16] As she puts it in her Preface, the Revolution must be seen as 'the natural consequence of intellectual improvement, gradually proceeding to perfection in the advancement of communities from a state of barbarism to that of polished society' (Wollstonecraft 1794: vii–viii). She asserts confidently in Book I Chapter i that

> Reason has, at last, shown her captivating face, beaming with benevolence; and it will be impossible for the dark hand of despotism to obscure its radiance, or the lurking dagger of subordinate tyrants to reach her bosom. The image of God implanted in our nature is now rapidly expanding . . .
> (Wollstonecraft 1794: 19)

and states that she intends to prove

> that the people are essentially good, and that knowledge is rapidly advancing to that degree of perfectibility, when the proud distinctions of sophisticating fools will be eclipsed by the mild rays of philosophy, and man may be considered as man – acting with the dignity of an intelligent being.
> (Wollstonecraft 1794: 72)

But many passages in the work make it clear that she is holding on to these beliefs only by means of a great intellectual effort in the face of the very different evidence offered by her observation and her feelings. In her Preface, indeed, she admits the difficulty, and the necessity of guarding against 'the erroneous inferences of sensibility' when confronted by

> The rapid changes, the violent, the base, and nefarious assassinations, which have clouded the vivid prospect that began to spread a ray of joy and gladness over the gloomy horizon of oppression, [and] cannot fail to chill the sympathizing bosom, and palsy intellectual vigour.
> (Wollstonecraft 1794: v–vi)

Her attempt to contemplate 'these stupendous events with the cool eye of observation' (Wollstonecraft 1794: vii) forces her to have recourse to various strategies in order to reconcile theory with practice. One of these, naturally enough, involves proving her first premise that the progress of reason and knowledge is in the direction of continual improvement. Since the example of the most recent events in France threatens to prove otherwise, she turns to the evidence of the past. In Book II Chapter iv, she sets out on a survey of world history which is intended to prove her point. As she chooses to begin with the pre-Christian era, she is forced to confront the fact that since

> all the improvements which were made in arts and sciences were suddenly overturned, both in Greece and in Rome . . . superficial reasoners have been led to think that there is only a certain degree of civilization to which men are capable of attaining, without receding back to a state of barbarism, by the horrid consequences of anarchy.
>
> (Wollstonecraft 1794: 219–220)

These ancient civilizations, she goes on to argue, 'never extended beyond polishing the manners, often at the expense of the heart, or morals'; and, moreover, the 'atrocious vices and gigantic crimes' which were committed at that period prove the progress of morality and reason (Wollstonecraft 1794: 223–226). She dismisses the Middle Ages as a period when 'Nothing . . . was founded on philosophical principles' (Wollstonecraft 1794: 230), and considers that although the Crusades 'freed many of the vassals' and that the clergy was much improved during the reformation, there was no substantial improvement in government (Wollstonecraft 1794: 231). Britain is, however, excepted, since the British constitution, although lacking a specific basis before 1688, rested on principles 'emanating from the consent, if not the sense, of the nation' (Wollstonecraft 1794: 232). The example of Britain, she points out, enabled America to form its own constitution (Wollstonecraft 1794: 234). In Europe, knowledge proceeded more slowly; but she recognises the advances in scientific knowledge made by Descartes and Newton as a factor in wearing away 'the ferocity of northern despotism' (Wollstonecraft 1794: 236–237), and she has nothing but praise for the court of Frederick the Great of Prussia as an example of the application of enlightened principles of knowledge and culture (Wollstonecraft 1794: 238). By this means she arrives at her final point, which is that France is the first European state to overthrow despotism, and thus represents the peak of progress so far (Wollstonecraft 1794: 239–240). She returns to the historical argument in her final chapter, where, under the heading 'The Progress of Reform', she argues that the development of the arts in France had softened the rigour of the old government, and allowed the philosophers to form a confederation, and to put together the Encyclopedia, which had 'eluded the dangerous vigilance of absolute ministers' (Wollstonecraft 1794: 496–498).

Even if Wollstonecraft's highly selective view of Western history is accepted, it is unfortunately clear that she is less certain of her proof than she at first appears. This is a result of the fact that although she feels certain that the overthrow of the despotic *ancien régime* represents an unarguable advance, the behaviour of the newly liberated French appears to disprove her arguments. She admits as much, indeed, in the conclusion of the work, which it is difficult not to see as a retraction of all the arguments about perfectibility and progress which have gone before:

> Let us examine the catalogue of vices of men in a savage state, and contrast them with those of men civilized; we shall find, that a barbarian, considered as a moral being, is an angel, compared with the refined villain of artificial life.
>
> (Wollstonecraft 1794: 521)

This inconsistency illustrates Wollstonecraft's chief difficulty in this work; the fact that, as she puts it in Book I Chapter iv,

> whilst the heart sickens over details of crimes and follies, and the understanding is appalled by the labour of unravelling a black tissue of plots, which exhibits the human character in the most revolting point of view, it is . . . difficult to bring ourselves to believe that out of this chaotic mass a fairer government is rising than has ever shed the sweets of social life on the world.
>
> (Wollstonecraft 1794: 73)

She makes various attempts to find a rational solution to this problem. The simplest is to be found in the continuation of this passage: 'But things must have time to find their level' (Wollstonecraft 1794: 73), or, as she puts it elsewhere, 'Things must be left to their natural course' (Wollstonecraft 1794: 345), since 'the improvements in philosophy and morals have been extremely tardy . . . [and] in the science of politics still more slow' (Wollstonecraft 1794: 396). This may not appear, at first glance, to offer a sufficient explanation for the fact that both the mobs and the newly elected Assembly have committed acts of atrocity, that

'disasters . . . have sullied the glories of the revolution' (Wollstonecraft 1794: 211), that men have behaved like 'monsters'
(Wollstonecraft 1794: 258), and that 'public anarchy, and private
discord, have been productive of . . . dreadful catastrophes and
wanton outrages' (Wollstonecraft 1794: 283). Wollstonecraft
blames two factors for this outcome, both of which are related to
what she sees as the precipitous speed with which events have
proceeded.

First, she offers an argument which had been central to her
Vindication of the Rights of Woman: if any section of society suffers
under a long period of oppression, its capacity for moral
development will be stunted. 'Just sentiments gain footing only
in proportion as the understanding is enlarged by cultivation'
(Wollstonecraft 1794: 126), and 'when men live in continual fear,
and know not what they have to apprehend, they always become
cunning and pusillanimous' (Wollstonecraft 1794: 138). Thus, the
French aristocracy have only themselves to blame; the rich have

> for ages tyrannized over the poor, teaching them how to act
> when possessed of power, and now they must feel the
> consequence. People are rendered ferocious by misery . . .
>   (Wollstonecraft 1794: 71)

Since she condemns 'the wild notions of original sin' (Wollstonecraft 1794: 17), and believes that 'the human heart is
naturally good' (Wollstonecraft 1794: 87), it follows that 'when
men once see . . . that on the general happiness depends their
own, reason will give strength to the fluttering wings of
passion . . .' (Wollstonecraft 1794: 15). Some external stimulus is
clearly needed for this result to take place, and freedom from
oppression, however desirable, is not in itself enough. Positive
social change – which in this case must originate from a
re-structuring of the system of government – is also required,
since 'the faculties of man are unfolded and perfected by the
improvements made to society' (Wollstonecraft 1794: 14).

It might be supposed that Wollstonecraft had grounds for
optimism on this count, given the fact that France had just
undergone enormous and fundamental political changes. But
although she sees the situation which existed in August 1789 as
'the point the most advantageous in which a government was
ever constructed', and is wholly in favour of the Declaration of
Rights (29 August), which she sees as evidence that 'reason was
tracing out the road which leads to virtue, glory and happiness'

(Wollstonecraft 1794: 297), she views many of the decisions made by the Assembly as, at best, rash and, at worst, disastrous.

Again, she blames the speed at which changes have been made:

> from the commencement of the revolution, the misery of France has originated from the folly or art of men, who have spurred the people on too fast; tearing up prejudices by the root, which they should have permitted to die away gradually.
>
> (Wollstonecraft 1794: 337)

She deplores the execution of Louis XVI, arguing that he should have been put into the care of another European monarchy, or allowed 'a small portion of liberty and power' (Wollstonecraft 1794: 340–1). While theoretically in favour of a republic, she argues that such a system is only suitable for a civilization which has reached a much higher degree of perfection than that so far attained by France (Wollstonecraft 1794: 344). She is unsympathetic to what she sees as the mistaken decision of the representatives not to form an upper chamber, which she believes would have acted as a check on the excesses of what she has earlier called 'desperate and impudent smatterers in politics' (Wollstonecraft 1794: 283); their fears that such a chamber would have become 'the asylum of a new aristocracy' can, she argues, 'only be accounted for by recollecting the many cruel thraldoms, from which they had so recently escaped' (Wollstonecraft 1794: 350). Instead of taking as their model Hume's Idea of a Perfect Commonwealth, an example which their present level of development rendered unsuitable because it represented too high an ideal to be immediately practicable – 'the revolution of states should be gradual' (Wollstonecraft 1794: 355) – she suggests that the French should have adopted a version of the American or the English plan (Wollstonecraft 1794: 356–7). She hastens to add that this need not lead to a condemnation of the theory itself as 'absurd and chimerical' (Wollstonecraft 1794: 357); she attributes the problem to the fact that too perfect and too difficult a model was fixed on too quickly.

All Wollstonecraft's best efforts at rationalisation are threatened with defeat, however, when her account reaches 5 October 1789, the occasion of the March of Women to Versailles, which she calls 'one of the blackest of the machinations that have since the revolution disgraced the dignity of man, and sullied the annals of humanity' (Wollstonecraft 1794: 449). Unable to conceive the probability that the women of Paris could have formed 'a plan so inhuman' by themselves, since, she says, they acted like 'a set of monsters, distinct from the people' (Wollstonecraft 1794: 450), she attributes the organisation of the march to the Duc d'Orléans. Her source for this supposition may have been the account of events which was published by the *Annual Register*:

> There are the strongest reasons for supposing, that the Orleans cabal, though assisted and supported by the republicans on very different grounds, were the immediate and principal authors of the present disturbances; none other could, in any degree, equally influence and command the rabble of that city, as the faction in question.[17]

The events of 5–6 October obviously affected Wollstonecraft powerfully; it is interesting to note that the strength of her reaction seems largely a result of what she sees as a desecration of the privacy of the king and queen, to which the massacre of the guards appears to take second place:

> The altar of humanity had been profaned – The dignity of freedom had been tarnished – The sanctuary of repose, the asylum of care and fatigue, the chaste temple of a woman, I consider the queen only as one . . . was violated in murderous fury – The life of the king was assailed, when he had acceded to all their demands – And, when their plunder was snatched from them, they massacred the guards, who were only doing their duty . . .
>
> (Wollstonecraft 1794: 457)

It would be easy to see this account, taken out of context, as wholly conservative – it could almost have come from the pen of Burke. The fact that it comes almost at the end of the volume possibly led Janet Todd to write of the *Historical and Moral View* that 'the second half . . . is harsher than the first'.[18] Passages throughout the book, however, clearly demonstrate that, for all her assertions to the contrary, Wollstonecraft's revulsion and despair frequently threaten to become stronger than her optimism.

In Book II Chapter ii, for example, she presents herself as weeping over the former oppressions of France, and eager to report the fall of the Bastille; but she is at once led to the recollection that the fortress is still used for 'the victims of revenge and suspicion', and her eulogy takes on a very different character from that which, presumably, she had originally intended:

> Down fell the temple of despotism; but – despotism has not been buried in its ruins! – Unhappy country! – when will thy children cease to tear thy bosom?
>
> (Wollstonecraft 1794: 163)

When she confines herself to a straighforward account of the events of 14 July, she manages for the most part to present them as 'a nation shaking off its fetters' (Wollstonecraft 1794: 182), 'a splendid example, to prove, that nothing can resist a people determined to live free' (Wollstonecraft 1794: 201); but the ambivalence of her attitude is made plain by the fact that these optimistic assertions are constantly undercut by indications that she is profoundly troubled. Her pleasure in the contemplation of 'the superiority of a nation rising in its own defence' is 'depressed by the recollection of the sinister events which have since clouded the bright beams' (Wollstonecraft 1794: 208); she is unable to forget the 'disasters [which] have sullied the glories of the revolution' and brought on 'the most fatal calamities' (Wollstonecraft 1794: 211); and although, she says, 'lively, sanguine minds' rejoiced when freedom rose up 'like a lion rouzed from his lair', the result has been the deplorable fact that 'the dogs of war have been let loose, and corruption has swarmed with noxious life' (Wollstonecraft 1794: 211). When she returns to the Fall of the Bastille, in Book III Chapter i, her support for violent change appears to have been eroded to such an extent that she now finds herself arguing that it might have been better if the fortress had not fallen at all:

> It is true, had the national assembly been allowed quietly to have made some reforms . . . the Bastille, though tottering on its dungeons, might yet have stood erect. – And if it had, the sum of human misery could scarcely have been in-creased. For the *guillotine* not finding it's way to the splendid square it had polluted, streams of innocent blood would not have flowed . . .
>
> (Wollstonecraft 1794: 251)[19]

Again, in Book V Chapter iii, she follows a passage in praise of the beauties of Paris with the reflection that 'this prospect of delights' quickly vanishes when one sees

The cavalcade of death [moving] along, shedding mildew over all the beauties of the scene, and blasting every joy! The elegance of the palaces is revolting, when they are viewed as prisons, and the sprightliness of the people disgusting, when they are hastening to view the operations of the guillo- tine, or carelessly passing over the earth stained with blood.

(Wollstonecraft 1794: 476)

Then, with 'bitterness of soul', the city is seen as 'a nest of crimes' – not, of course, the crimes of the *ancien régime*, but those of the present government. Other examples of the same kind can be found throughout the book. Indeed, if the work is read carefully, it becomes difficult to see why twentieth-century commentators have described Wollstonecraft's attitude as optimistic.[20]

The fact that Wollstonecraft's declared object was a survey of the origin as well as the progress of the Revolution, and that she set out to provide a moral view in addition to a historical one, led to the fact that by the end of her volume of 522 pages, her account had reached only as far as 19 October 1789. Nevertheless, her perspective is unavoidably coloured by the fact that she was writing in the middle of 1793, with all the added wisdom of hindsight. Certainly a comparison of the reaction of other expatri- ate observers at this period suggests that until at least 1792 it was possible to view in a remarkably optimistic light occurences which would later seem to point forward to the excesses of Robespierre and the Reign of Terror. The British travel writer Arthur Young, for example, who had written in his *Travels During the Years 1787, 1788 and 1789* (1792) that 'the extent and universal- ity of oppression under which the people groaned' was such that 'a revolution was . . . absolutely necessary to the welfare of the kingdom' (539–40), was so shocked by the events of 1792 and early 1793 that he took the opposite view in his next work, *The Example of France a Warning to Britain* (1793):

[The Revolution] has brought more misery, poverty, devas- tation, imprisonment, bloodshed, and ruin on France, in four years, than the old government did in a century . . . [it] has absolutely ruined the kingdom . . . the old government of France, with all its faults, was certainly the best enjoyed by any considerably [sic] country in Europe.

(13–14, 35, 36)

Helen Maria Williams, who had lived in France since July 1790, had strenuously asserted in the first volume of her *Letters Written in France* (1790) that the rumours reaching England of 'crimes, assassinations, torture and death' were greatly exaggerated, and that although reflections on the bloodshed gave rise to 'gloomy images' she felt that gains had been made at 'a far cheaper rate than could have been expected' (Williams 1790: 16–217, 81–82). However, she too was forced by 1793 to speak of 'anarchy', of 'sanguinary rites', of 'infernal executions', and of the 'deep and extraordinary malignity' of Robespierre', although she continued to assert that *'the foundation was laid in wisdom'* (Williams 1793: iii [17], iv, 269).

Another, though admittedly *ex post facto*, account was given by William Wordsworth, who – as a convinced anti-monarchist – had arrived in Paris on 29 October 1792 on his way back to England from Orleans. He describes his mood at the time as one in which 'enflamed with hope', he viewed the crimes perpetrated in the name of the Revolution as 'Ephemeral monsters, to be seen but once,/Things that could only shew themselves and die'.[21] Nevertheless, his account of the unexpected turmoil of mind which he experienced during his first night in Paris is remarkably similar to the imaginative confusion described a few months later in Wollstonecraft's December letter to Johnson:

> I thought of those September massacres,
> Divided from me by a little month,
> And felt and touched them, a substantial dread . . .
> 'The horse is taught his manage, and the wind
> Of heaven wheels round and treads in his own steps;
> Year follows year, the tide returns again,
> Day follows day, all things have second birth;
> The earthquake is not satisfied at once' –
> And in such way I wrought upon myself,
> Until I seemed to hear a voice that cried
> To the whole city, 'Sleep no more!'
> (Wordsworth 1805: x, 64–76)

Wordsworth's doubts and fears over the course of the next two years – the deep divisions created in his mind by England's declaration of war with France, the 'melancholy' days and disturbed nights which he experienced during the Reign of Terror, his exultation at hearing of the death of Robespierre, and his subsequent disappointment when the 'golden times' which he hoped would succeed failed to materialise – are all described in detail in the 1805 *Prelude* Book x. He concludes his account by describing how, much in need of a new source of philosophical optimism, he turned to Godwin's *Political Justice*, since, he says, he still 'had hope to see/ . . . The man to come parted as by a gulph/ From him who had been' (Wordsworth 1805: xi, 58–60) – a hope which was vitally relevant at a period when the man 'who had been', in revolutionary France, at least, had shown himself capable of inconceivable atrocities. Thus, as Hazlitt wrote, 'No work in our time gave such a blow to the philosophical mind of the country as the celebrated *Enquiry Concerning Political Justice*'.[22] Clearly, this effect was largely attributable to Godwin's certainties about man's ultimate perfectibility. His confident assertion that

> It requires no great degree of fortitude to look with indifference on the false fire of the moment and to forsee the calm period of reason which will succeed.[23]

offered a tempting antidote to the intellectual confusion which was, increasingly, assailing supporters of revolutionary principles.

It is, of course, noticeable that Wollstonecraft's attempts to counteract her own growing confusion and despair rest mainly on assertions of the ultimate perfectibility of mankind and of political systems, which receive greater emphasis in this work than in any of her previous writings. The publication of *Political Justice*, in February 1793, coincided with Wollstonecraft's deep depression and loss of faith, demonstrated in her 'Letter: Introductory' (composed the same month). Since she was undoubtedly kept supplied with books and literary magazines by her friends in England, it would be tempting to speculate that she read Godwin's book – or at least a review of the work[24] – during the spring or early summer of 1793, and that its optimistic philosophy enabled her to attempt the more positive view of events which she embarked upon in June of that year. Such a theory of influence, however, convenient and attractive though it would be, is impossible to prove. Even passages from the *Historical and Moral View* which appear to be resoundingly Godwinian, such as the assertion that

> Reason has at last shown her captivating face, beaming with benevolence; and it will be impossible for the dark hand of despotism again to obscure its radiance, or the lurking dagger of tyrants to reach her bosom . . .
>
> (Wollstonecraft 1794: 19)

could be attributed to a common source in the literature of rational dissent, to which both Godwin and Wollstonecraft owed much of their thinking.[25]

At all events, whatever the stimulus was for Wollstonecraft's attempt to present an optimistic and positive view of the events in France, it proved to be only fitfully and temporarily effective. Her declared intention, in the Preface, of exercising 'the cool eye of observation' (Wollstonecraft 1794: vii), led – as the *British Critic* astutely pointed out – to conclusions which frequently acted in complete opposition to her declared 'first principles'. In spite of assertions to the contrary by commentators from Godwin on-wards, it is my belief that Wollstonecraft's faith in Revolution principles never entirely recovered from the first shock of despair which her 'Letter: Introductory' makes plain. This seems to be confirmed by a passage in her *Letters . . . in . . . Sweden*:

> An ardent affection for the human race makes enthusiastic characters eager to produce alteration in laws and govern-ments prematurely. To render them useful and permanent, they must be the growth of each particular soil, and the gradual fruit of the ripening understanding of the nation, matured by time, not forced by an unnatural fermentation.[26]

In many ways the logical outcome of her insistence, in the *Historical and Moral View*, that change must take place slowly, this passage nevertheless suggests that her thinking had moved on by this time to the point where she was able to admit – as she had been unable to do two years earlier – that violent upheavals, such as had taken place in France, were never to be desired.

References

1. Hereafter cited as Wollstonecraft 1794. No further volumes of this work appeared.
2. Wardle, R.M. (1951). *Mary Wollstonecraft: A Critical Biography*. London and Kansas, University of Kansas Press, (hereafter cited as Wardle 1951), 212.
3. See Janes, R.M. (1978). 'On the Reception of Mary Wollstonecraft's *A Vindication of the Rights of Woman*', *Journal of the History of Ideas*, 39, 293–302.
4. (1796). *Critical Review; or Annals of Literature*, xvi, 391.
5. (1794). *Analytical Review, or History of Literature, Domestic and Foreign*, xx, 337. Wollstonecraft had been employed as a reviewer by the *Analytical* since 1787.

6. (1795). *Monthly Review; or Literary Journal*, n.s. xvi, 393–402.
7. See Sullivan, A. (ed.) (1983). *British Literary Magazines: The Romantic Age 1789–1836*, Westport, Conn., and London, Greenwood, 57–62. Nares and Below appear also to have been responsible for all the articles and reviews.
8. (1795). *British Critic*, vi, 36.
9. To Eliza W. Bishop. Wardle, R.M. (ed.) (1979). *Collected Letters of Mary Wollstonecraft*. Ithaca and London, Cornell University Press, (hereafter cited as Wardle 1979), 231.
10. The trip had originally been planned in June 1792, at which time it was intended that the Fueslis and Johnson would also go. Wollstonecraft wrote then to her sister that 'I shall be introduced to many people, my book has been translated and praised in the popular prints . . . we intend to be absent only six weeks' (To Everina Wollstonecraft, 20 June 1792. Wardle 1979: 213).
11. See for example the popular works by Helen Maria Williams: (1790). *Letters on the French Revolution, written in France, in the Summer of 1790*, London, Robinson (hereafter cited as Williams 1790); (1792) 2nd edn., 2 vols.; (1793). Vols. iii and iv (hereafter cited as Williams 1793); and Arthur Young: (1792). *Travels During the Years 1787, 1788 and 1789*, Bury St. Edmunds, W. Richardson.
12. (1798), 4 vols. London, J. Johnson, iv, 39–51 (hereafter cited as Wollstonecraft 1793).
13. Godwin, W. (1798) *Memoirs of the Author of 'A Vindication of the Rights of Woman'*. London, J. Johnson, (hereafter cited as Godwin 1798) 101, 102.
14. (1791). *Letter to the Right Honourable Edmund Burke, Occasioned by his Reflections on the Revolution in France*. Birmingham, T. Pearson, 147.
15. (1790) *Observations on the Reflections of the Rt. Hon. Edmund Burke . . . in a Letter to the Rt. Hon. Earl of Stanhope*. London, C. Dilly, 20.
16. For a full discussion of millenarianism at this period see Garrett, C. (1975). *Respectable Folly: Millenarians and the French Revolution in France and England*. Baltimore and London, Johns Hopkins University Press.
17. (1793). *The Annual Register, or a View of the History, Politics and Literature for the Year 1790*, 47.
18. Todd, J.M. (1976). *Mary Wollstonecraft: An Annotated Bibliography*. New York and London, Garland, 4.
19. According to Godwin, Wollstonecraft had been deeply disturbed by a first-hand experience of the guillotine: 'Before she left Paris for Neuilly, she happened one day to enter Paris on foot . . . when an execution, attended with some peculiar aggravations, had just taken place, and the blood of the guillotine appeared fresh upon the pavement. The emotions of her soul burst forth in indignant exclamations, while a prudent bystander warned her of her danger, and intreated her to hasten and hide her discontents.' (Godwin 1798: 116).

20. See Todd, J.M. (ed.) (1975). Mary Wollstonecraft: *An Historical and Moral View*, Scholars' Facsimiles and Reprints. New York and London, Garland, 11; Wardle 1951: 206.

21. (1805). *The Prelude* (hereafter cited as Wordsworth 1805) x, 37–39.

22. Howe, P.P. (ed.) (1930–34). *The Complete Works of William Hazlitt*, 21 vols. London and Toronto, Dent, xi, 17.

23. Godwin, W., (1793). *An Enquiry Concerning Political Justice, and its Influence on General Virtue and Happiness*, 2 vols., London, Robinson, i, p. xii.

24. *Political Justice* was reviewed in the *Analytical* in June and August 1793 (vol. xvi, 121–130, 388–404).

25. For an intelligent discussion of the sources of Godwin's thought, see Philp, M. (1986). *Godwin's Political Justice*. London, Duckworth, 15–79, (and ibid. 175–192 for Wollstonecraft's possible influence on Godwin's changing attitudes to 'sensual commerce' and to marriage). Wollstonecraft was certainly familiar with *Political Justice* by August 1796, when she referred to it ironically in a note to Godwin (Wardle 1979: 339–40). Since, however, she was by this time involved in a relationship with him, this does not help one to decide whether her renewed interest in Godwin, whom she had initially disliked (see Godwin 1798: 93–7) had been owing to her admiration for his work, or whether she had read his work as a result of their developing relationship.

26. (1796) *Letters Written During a Short Residence in Sweden, Norway, and Denmark*. London, J. Johnson, Appendix [264].

Mark Hatenboer

6

The limits of Paine's revolutionary literalism

John Whale

In his acceptance speech for the Republican presidential nomination in 1980 Ronald Reagan invoked the figure of Tom Paine writing 'in the darkest days of the American Revolution'. *Common Sense* provided him with the rhetoric with which to launch the revolution of 'Reaganomics': 'we have it in our power to begin the world over again' (Paine 1973: 59). The words echoed eerily in the nuclear arms negotiations and 'star wars' debates that followed. That Reagan's appropriation of Paine might seem surprising as well as frightening to some on the Left suggests that as much attention should be given to analysing the ideological grounds of Paine's texts as to chronicling his role in the successes of Enlightenment rationalism.[1] Nowhere are these grounds more evident than in his literalist attack on the 'artistry' of Burke's *Reflections* in *Rights of Man*. Their debate about the French Revolution exposes a crisis of representation in which there is a fundamental difference as to the definition of truth and art. Despite the ideological collusion deriving from the fact that each text owes its own kind of allegiance to the formation of a bourgeois revolution, account must also be taken of the surface difference which produced the political debate of the 1790s.[2] This difference between Burke's *Reflections* and *Rights of Man* is inseparable from that of ideology. It is precisely this coexistence of ideological collusion with representational difference which is politically important and historically revealing. Otherwise it is impossible to account for the diverse appropriations of Paine which have taken place: as revolutionary, seditious pamphleteer, popular philosopher, champion of liberalism and father of American independence. Without an awareness of the specific identity of Paine's mode of representation, such powerful appropriations as Reagan's will always come as a disabling shock.

Exploration of Paine's writings reveals a deep-rooted suspicion of the imaginative faculty. Fictional or symbolic status is not seen as an alternative to, but as a distortion of, rational reality. Imaginative fantasy or projection, rather than being validated as a higher order of knowledge, as in Keats's idea of 'negative capability', cannot be dissociated from deception. When in *The Age of Reason* imagination is accused of both unreality and distortion, Paine's demystification of it is intent on making it look ridiculous – not to draw attention to a perspective from which it might look so, but that the ridiculous is intrinsic to it. The suggestion is that not only is true seriousness altogether lost, but that in the act of imagination the mind has become a travesty of itself. Within Paine's class confrontation 'refined' entertainment is at one with imagination: its typical characteristics are variety, diversity and copiousness. Left unchecked it sports with numerous impossibilities, released at last from the constraints of truth. The necessary check upon this sportive fancy, that which keeps it in touch with reason, is provided by a 'serene mind' and a 'happy philosophical temperament'. Here the strength of the sound mind means that it can afford to play with thought, calmly dictate to it, rather than allow it to amuse itself and thereby fall foul of its own riotous inclination. The happiness of the philosopher is often seen to be the result of temperament in Paine, not just a result of rational control. The inference is very strong that not only does the imagination's playfulness dislocate it from truth, but that its chaotic anarchy of rival fictions is the product of an unhappy mind. In this respect Burke's *Reflections* are the inevitably disordered product of a mind feeding on the divisiveness of fear, rather than depending on the harmonious force of benevolence.

This general attack on invention explains Paine's dismissive attitude to language. According to *The Age of Reason*, the history of a religious event in language is a history of its degradation and obscurity. Through this process of travesty it begins to look more like fiction. Religious history becomes mere fable instead of parable. As a result Paine laments the lack of a universal language which would purify scripture of imprecision and changeability. 'Language cannot convey either the idea or the word of God' because of 'the want of a universal language'; scripture is subject to 'the mutability of language; the errors to which translators are subject; the possibility of altering it, or of fabricating the whole, and imposing it upon the world' (Paine 1969: iv 83). His response to what we might call fallen language is to displace it altogether. He switches from text to 'Nature' and makes the latter a language. By what seems like a metaphorical sleight-of-hand Paine short-circuits the problem of representation. Both the terms and the method of this procedure are characteristic of his work: the idealistic drive and the polemical success of his arguments depend on this kind of out-facing tactic. It is equivalent to moving behind the enemy lines. Anteriority is the key position in this war of origins. In his arguments on origins, in his geometric metaphors of straight lines, and in his debates on the body politic, Paine's radical individualism depends on some unexpected values, and his extreme literalism rests on some disturbingly 'natural' and metaphysical grounds.

I

Paine's texts are struck between two loyalties: a belief in progress and an adherence to origins. The conflict between these two is apparent in his arguments with Burke over the definition of 'revolution'. When the squabble over precedents hots up in *Rights of Man*, Tom Paine goes straight for Burke's philosophical affiliations and turns the argument into one of origins instead. In doing so he immediately short-circuits the whole of history which now stands forlorn, as a rather inadequate product of human invention. He makes the image of the chasm rebound on its author by challenging Burke on the so-called revolution of 1688: 'It was government dethroning government; and the old one, by attempting to make a new one, made a chasm' (Paine 1982: 124). He does so in typical fashion, claiming that his adversary's argument is paradoxical. That which is paradoxical is also impossible or fictional, it is assumed. Similarly, in the aptly titled 'Prospects on the Rubicon', Paine refers his reader to the chaos in pre-revolutionary French society, though in this instance the chaos is real and necessary, unlike the contrived chasm which derives from Burke's aesthetics. As a result, it is given the sanction of original authority, despite being a form of disorder:

> While this change is working there will appear a kind of chaos in the nation; but the creation we enjoy arose out of

chaos, and our greatest blessings appear to have a confused beginning.

(Paine 1969: ii 206)

By attempting to account positively for a form of disorder, Paine is, for once, betrayed into a penchant for obscurity, the very thing for which he castigates Burke, antithetical as it is to his own belief in the clear light of reason. For the most part, however, Paine finds success in exposing the 'chasm' of Burke's text, the paradoxical emptiness of which has been produced by artifice:

> It is not among the least of the evils of the present existing governments in all parts of Europe, that man, considered as man, is thrown back to a vast distance from his Maker, and the artificial chasm filled up by a succession of barriers or sort of turnpike gates, through which he has to pass . . . the duty of man is not a wilderness of turnpike gates, through which he has to pass by tickets from one to the other. It is plain and simple.

(Paine 1969: 89)

The object of Paine's levelling rationalism is to regain the blissful seat of unmediated knowledge. The laying low of the barriers of superstition – whether in the realms of religion or politics (for both are in this respect related), prepares the ground for a new beginning only in the sense of restoring an original order. Paine's claim, in *Rights of Man*, of a 'regeneration' thus figures as an appropriately religious term.[3] Paradoxically, the moral imperative which enables a revolutionary new start can never entirely escape its own origins and allow a clean break for the secularised world of free trade and commerce – that other kingdom for which Paine has such high hopes.

The conflict in Paine's writing between progression and a reverence for a lost origin derives in part from context. Certainly, the clash between these two is something of a commonplace in eighteenth-century thought, and figures prominently, for example, in Rousseau where it takes the form of a contest between the noble savage and the alienating sophistication of society. The conflict is not simply between past and present. That lost Eden might figure prominently, but it is lost and figures now as a trope which defines the perception of the present. In Paine's case the search for origins comes about under pressure from the peculiar power of Burke's text, or the chaos of the present political turmoil of American independence, or the French revolution. Faced with the chaos of text or event in these instances, Paine's appeal to origins is both a philosophical ploy in keeping with his persona and an attempt at re-orientation. Faced with the bewildering variety of the Bible in *The Age of Reason* (a variety which is characteristic of imagination), Paine makes the following plea: 'Search not written or printed books, but the Scripture called the CREATION . . . Man cannot make or invent, or contrive principles: he can only discover them' (Paine 1969: iv 239).

That this kind of appeal is a peculiar and necessary response to crisis is made apparent in the following extract from 'The Forester's Letters' (1775):

> Whoever will take the trouble of attending to the changeability of times and things, and the conduct of mankind thereon, will find that EXTRAORDINARY CIRCUMSTANCES do sometimes rise before us, of a species, either so purely natural or so perfectly original that none but the man of nature can understand them. When precedents fail to spirit us, we must return to the first principles of things for information; and THINK as if we were the FIRST MEN that THOUGHT and this is the true reason that, in the present state of affairs, the wise are 'become foolish, and the foolish wise'.
>
> (Paine 1969: i 154–155)

Even here of course – in the very claim of an unprecedented event – Paine is politically committed. The case of the French Revolution makes it perfectly clear that one of the attempts of the forces of reaction was to tame it by making it conform to a pre-existing category. In this particular instance Paine gives a good indication of the way in which the appeal to origins is capable of reversing categories, of turning everything upside-down. It possesses the ability to make accepted reality appear paradoxical. Much of the power of his own writing, of course, comes from precisely this aim of making an established argument look contradictory. It is certainly the basis of his strategy in dealing with Burke and the Bible.

By way of exposing the lack of method in Burke's *Reflections*, Paine anecdotally offers the reader the following geographical analogy. As he points to the vacuity of Burke's work he is led to contemplate the nature of paradox. The irony is that he cannot simply dismiss it as an empty hoax: instead he has to read through it, and thereby allow it to make its imprint on his own text. What he describes as a delusory walk upon the shore turns out to be the very thing which dictates the crab-like nature of his own attack:

> I know a place in America called Point-no-Point, because as you proceed along the shore, gay and flowery as Mr Burke's language, it continually recedes and presents itself at a distance before you; but when you have got as far as you can go, there is no point at all. Just thus it is with Mr Burke's three hundred and fifty-six pages. It is therefore difficult to reply to him. But as the point he wishes to establish, may be inferred from what he abuses, it is in his paradoxes that we must look for his arguments.
>
> (Paine 1982: 71)

That Paine focusses here on what he sees as the disorientating effect of Burke's language is not fortuitous: it is supported by frequent metaphors and analogies which stress Burke's waywardness and his own direction. As we have already seen, he considers the Abbé Raynal's work on the American revolution to be possessed of the same unfortunate imaginative luxuriance. As a result, it too is capable of leading the reader astray and masking the fact with its intoxicating pleasure: the Abbé's writings are 'uncentral and burdened with variety. They represent a beautiful wilderness without paths; in which the eye is diverted by every thing without being particularly directed to any thing; and in which it is agreeable to be lost, and difficult to find the way out' (Paine 1969: ii 110). Clearly, the censure is not without a puritanical foundation; a fear of temptation assailing through the senses, and taking place in a convenient wilderness. As Paine proceeds to 'follow Mr Burke through a pathless wilderness of rhapsodies' (Paine 1982: 86), the effect of the exposé is to generate ridicule from the superior vantage-point of rationality rather than moral condemnation from an indignant sense of self-righteousness. It is a common tactic in many an eighteenth-century anti-luxury text. The convenient thing as far as Paine is concerned is that the arrogant superiority of his position can be easily combined with popularity. That is its real power. As he argues in 'Letters to American Citizens': 'the right will always become the popular if it has courage to show itself, and the shortest way is always a straight line' (Paine 1969: iii 401).

II

Confronted with the chaos of political crisis or the variety of the artistic text, Paine draws on the analogy of the straight line. It can be conveniently used to connect his belief in geometry and his belief in individualism: it can be made to fit with the universal laws of nature and with the individual's intervention on behalf of social enlightenment. This is particularly apparent in the *Crisis Papers* where the analogy is frequently ushered in to support the overall attempt to stabilise and mobilise opinion on behalf of independence. The straight line thus figures as natural law and individual experience. As we have already seen, in his critique of Burke's *Reflections*, where, it is claimed, turnpikes have been placed in the way of nature, Paine's straight lines frequently take the form of metaphors of the road. The obstructions created by Burke's artifice represent a degradation of nature and a distancing of the individual from God or the world of his creation. On a more practical level, of course, such barriers cut him/her off from their rights; or more practically still, as the analogy itself suggests, from the benefits of free trade. Where the contrast needs to be more extreme, Paine switches the metaphor slightly and contrasts the journey by road with the uncertainty of a voyage by sea: the singleness of a journey by land is compared with the alarming prospect of a plural ocean. Like Burke's *Reflections*, the Bible itself merits this description: 'Is it not more safe that we stop ourselves at the plain, pure, and unmixed belief of one God, which is deism, than that we commit ourselves on an ocean of improbable, irrational, indecent, and contradictory tales?' (Paine 1969: iv 156).

When Paine connects his attack on the variety of imagination with these metaphors which contain a latent plot, it is evident that the threatened response of the reader is being considered. Instead of being idly amused with the multiplicity of objects that go to make up a refined aesthetic experience, the spectator or reader, according to Paine, should be disconcerted, ill-at-ease or, at the least, confused. His strategy is to undermine the leisured position guaranteed by the authority of 'good taste'. By applying reason to make it look chaotic and inconsistent, Paine also makes it look frantic and disordered.

But though Paine's metaphors seem to promise a plot, they function mainly on a spatial level. The system of metaphors we have been looking at seems to serve merely as a pivot between progress and adherence to origins. The resultant indeterminacy is particularly disconcerting since the liberating potential of these straight lines is so compelling; as, for instance, in the following statement:

> The genuine mind of man, thirsting for its native home, society, condemns the gewgaws that separate him from it. Titles are like circles drawn by the magician's wand, to contract the sphere of man's felicity. He lives immured in the Bastille of a word, and surveys at a distance the envied life of man.
>
> (Paine 1982: 102)

That these potentially liberating lines are really severed from time and history becomes apparent when the nature of principles is explained: for these lines turn out to be either manifestations of, or the quickest routes through to, rather mysterious 'principles'.

In 'First Principles of Government' Paine seems to suggest that the straight line as opposed to the imprisoning circle is in accord with origins: 'It is by tracing things to their origin that we learn to understand them: and it is by keeping that line and that origin always in view that we never forget them' (Paine 1969: iii 271). The problem here, of course, is in deciding the extent to which the two are separate: is Paine suggesting that we keep both the origin and the access to it clear in our minds? For the extent to which they are separate is important in determining whether a scheme of history is involved in the evolution of such principles. Two further statements from the same work would suggest that there is some conflict on this issue. When Paine challenges the idea of heredity becoming a right through usage, he is prepared to dismiss time (in the sense of custom) as a valid criterion by which to judge of right.

> This would be supposing an absurdity; for either it is putting time in the place of principle, or making it superior to principle; whereas time has no more connection with, or influence upon principle, than principle has upon time. The wrong which began a thousand years ago, is as much wrong as if it began today; and the right which originates today, is as much a right as if it had the sanction of a thousand years. Time with respect to principles is an eternal NOW: it has no operation upon them: it changes nothing of their nature and qualities. But what have we to do with a

thousand years? Our life-time is but a short portion of that period, and if we find the wrong in existence as soon as we begin to live, that is the point of time at which it begins to us; and our right to resist it is the same as if it never existed before.

(Paine 1969: iii 260)

From this it is clear that the insurrectionary force of his writings derives not only from the attack on precedents, but also from a much more inclusive assault on the category of time itself. With each new generation time begins anew; history is forgotten, but the eternal principles are forever kept in view by the straight lines of reason. In contrast to this clear-cut statement for the political activist, Paine later makes greater concessions to the force of custom and usage. The gradualist approach evident in the following passage is at least aware of the recalcitrant nature of the popular consciousness when faced with revolutionary change. For once commonsense is not immediate and transparent:

> There never was any truth or any principle so irresistibly obvious that all men believed it at once. Time and reason must cooperate with each other to the final establishment of any principle; and therefore those who may happen to be first convinced have not a right to persecute others, on whom conviction has operated more slowly. The moral principle of revolutions is to construct, not to destroy.
>
> (Paine 1969: iii 277)

Although the process of his own true principles is still seen as inevitable (just slower) in this statement, there is at least a grudging awareness of the slavish power of opinion. So here we have two conflicting, though not strictly contradictory, ideas of time as it affects Paine's eternal principles. The latter are separate from considerations of time and place; yet duration and practical application are required for them to take effect. (One assumes in the foregoing quotation that 'establishment' is not synonymous with 'formation'.) If this concern with time and its relationship with principle is considered more particularly with regard to Paine's idea of each generation legislating for itself, the same conflict emerges. When he asserts that 'The rights of men in society, are neither divisible, nor transferrable, nor annihilable, but are descendable only; and it is not in the power of any generation to intercept finally, and cut off the descent' (Paine 1982: 146), Paine invokes again the passage of a single straight line leading back to the originating principles which guarantee universal rights. He might well be doing for the rights of man exactly what he denies to the property and heredity rights of Burke's patriarchal system; but in advocating a line of continuity at all, he puts in motion an idea which clashes with the right of each generation to 'begin the world over again' (Paine 1973: 59).

If, in the main, the principles to which Paine refers are eternal and universal, the time scheme they suggest is an 'eternal now'. It is not surprising, therefore, that history should look inadequate or ridiculous: according to these principles history can only be the telling of stories; and, as a result, all narrative structures begin to look redundant.

III

At least, this is so until we consider another aspect of Paine's writings, and one which leads to entrances onto the stage of politics. That aspect is Paine's awareness of man as a physical, decaying body. As in many a case of eighteenth-century rationalism, the idealisms of an unageing intellect are matched by a particularly acute awareness of the dying animal.

Hereditary kingship is attacked throughout Paine's political writings, and is responsible for generating two strands of thought in his work: the investigation of the relationship between generations and the exploration of the individual. In the case of the latter, Paine's egalitarianism leads to the articulation of a new form of individualism and a new way of looking at the body. Despite the extremes of the debate, both strands are controlled by the prevailing economic mode of thought. In order to combat Burke's idea of hereditary succession to entailed property, Paine puts the body in the place of property; according to his self-proclaimed egalitarianism, the mature free agent now replaces the entailed child. From the very beginning of his career, with the anti-slavery essay, Paine reacts strongly against the right of property invading the person, 'The base idea of man having property in man' (Paine 1982: 104). That his interest in the body is at least partly inspired by economics is immediately apparent in the following declaration from 'First Principles of Government'. Having described the person as 'sacred' his attention is very soon turned to a different sort of value:

> The protection of a man's person is more sacred than the protection of property; and besides this, the facility of

performing any kind of work or services by which he ac-
quires a livelihood, or maintaining a family, is of the nature
of property. It is property to him; he has acquired it; and it
is as much the object of his protection as exterior property,
possessed without that faculty, can be the object of property in another person.

> (Paine 1969: 269)

Clearly, Paine is not so much interested in arguing for the in-
violable rights of the private individual as in extending the way
in which the individual – even his/her body and its labour – is
situated in relation to production, an aspect of political economy
which was to interest Cobbett as well as Marx and Engels. (In
this he is at least as thoroughgoing as Burke.) Similarly, when
he comes to consider the origin and the right of representative
government in the same work, it is a case of transferring the language of property to the body: 'Man is himself the origin and the
evidence of the right, it appertains to him in right of his existence, and his person is the title deed' (Paine 1969: iii 264–265).
Man has not property in man, but each man has the rights of
property in himself as long as he shall live.

On the same principle, Paine argues, must each generation
function. It has the rights of its existence, but when that lapses
so do the rights: 'The vanity and presumption of governing
beyond the grave is the most ridiculous and insolent of all tyran-
nies. Man has no property in man, neither has one generation a
property in the generations that are to follow' (Paine 1969:
iii 263). According to this idea, properly disinterested legislation
has no hold beyond the limits of natural life. In 'The Eighteenth
Fructidor' Paine comments: 'The Constitution in this respect, is
as impartially constructed as if those who framed it were to die
as soon as they had finished their work' (Paine 1969: iii 349).
From what we have already seen of eternal principles, those
other respects not referred to are clearly important. Paine is
equally aware of the dangers. He is alert to the absurdity and
difficulty of a system in which, as he puts it, 'Every new election
would be a new revolution, or it would suppose the public of
the former year dead and a new public in its place' (Paine 1969: ii
147–148).

Even so, his depiction of the nation in 'First Principles of
Government' focusses on the difficulty of finding a still point
from which legislation can be legitimate. (He resolves the same

problem in his own prose by addressing it to the mature reader.)[4] The problem in characterising the nation is that it is forever on the move – at different stages between birth and death:

> A nation, though continually existing is continually in a state of renewal and succession. It is never stationary. Every day produces new births, carries minors forward to maturity, and old persons from the stage. In this ever running flood of generations there is no point superior in authority to another. Could we conceive an idea of superiority in any, at what point of time, or in what century are we to ascribe it? By what evidence are we to prove it? By what criterion are we to know it? A single reflection will teach us that our ancestors like ourselves were but tenants for life in the great freehold of rights.
>
> (Paine 1969: iii 261–262)

At the very point where it seems that his sense of urgency makes it impossible to act provisionally, along comes the familiar revelation of truth – a truth expressed once more in the language of property.

It is this strong sense of human mortality which clashes so strongly with Burke's ideas of heredity. According to Paine, Burke offends against the very nature of man's existence with all its religious resonances. Strangely, the logic of Paine's argument is that in denying the inevitability of death, Burke denies the fact of life: in going against 'the nature of man' he has effected an 'annihilation'. He has set up his own creation in defiance of the creator:

> It is the nature of man to die, and he will continue to die as long as he continues to be born. But Mr Burke has set up a sort of political Adam, in which all posterity are bound forever; he must therefore prove that his Adam possessed such a power or such a right.
>
> (Paine 1982: 66)

Burke's Adam is an unnatural monster (unlike his more famous cousins in the period) who works on the side of 'imprisonment' while claiming divine sanction.

In his relentless opposition to kingship, Paine attempts to set up a form of government which overcomes the inconsistencies and caprices of the individual and even of single generations. More and more it appears that it is government which is able to uphold his rights of 'man', overcome the tyranny of the body, and transcend this mortal state. Representative government, Paine argues,

> places government in a state of constant maturity. It is, as has been already stated, never young, never old. It is subject neither to nonage or dotage. It is never in the cradle nor on crutches. It admits not of separation between knowledge and power, and is superior, as government ought to be, to all the accidents of individual man, and is therefore superior to what is called monarchy.
>
> (Paine 1982: 203)

At this point Paine makes explicit the difference between his ideal system and the body, and, more particularly, highlights the inappropriateness of the analogy. The body is supplanted by geometry:

> A nation is not a body, the figure of which is to be represented by the human body; but is like a body in which every radius meets; and that centre is formed by representation. To connect representation with what is called monarchy, is eccentric government. Representation is of itself the delegated monarchy of a nation, and cannot debase itself by dividing it with another.
>
> (Paine 1982: 203)

This might appear very similar to Burke's strategy – a way of maintaining continuity by overcoming death. It too looks like an attempt to put the idealisms of 'man' beyond nature.

When Bishop Watson responds to Paine's *The Age of Reason* in his *Apology for the Bible*, he argues vehemently on behalf of hereditary succession and describes it rather luridly in terms of the body politic. According to Watson, it is precisely the civilised virtues and their maintenance through inheritance which stand opposed to the unseemly fact of death. Clearly, there is a different kind of religious transposition going on here: relations of property are made sacred; by inheritance death is conquered. Even if one doesn't make a link between 'common stock' and the 'fetid mass of corruption', Watson's allegiances are fairly clear, his values threatened:

> One of the principal rights of man, in a state either of nature or of society, is a right of property in the fruits of his industry, ingenuity or good fortune. Does government hold any

man in ignorance of this right? So much the contrary, that the chief care of government is to declare, ascertain, modify, and defend this right; nay, it gives the right, where nature gives none; it protects the goods of an intestate; and it allows a man, at his death, to dispose of that property which the law of nature would cause to revert into the common stock. Sincerely as I am attached to the liberties of mankind, I cannot but profess myself an utter enemy to that spurious philosophy, that democratic insanity which would equalise all property, and level all distinctions in civil society. Personal distinctions, arising from superior probity, learning, eloquence, skill, courage, and from every other excellence of talents, are the very blood and nerves of the body politic: they animate the whole, and invigorate every part; without them, its bones would become reeds, and its marrow water; it would presently sink into a fetid mass of corruption.

(Watson 1984: 111–112)

As one might expect, Rousseau is closer to Paine on this issue. In the 'Discourse on Political Economy' he too had been sceptical about using the body metaphor to describe the system of government: 'I shall take the liberty of making use of a very common, and in some respects inaccurate comparison' (Rousseau 1973: 120). Significantly, when he addresses the issue again, in *Du Contrat Social*, it is under the chapter heading 'The Death of the Body Politic'. Here there is that same sense of mortality and the impulse to see government as a means of overcoming it, which we have seen in Paine. At this point he too has to contend with the conflict between nature and artifice:

The body politic, as well as the human body, begins to die as soon as it is born, and carries in itself the causes of its destruction. But both may have a constitution that is more or less robust and suited to preserve them a longer or a shorter time. The constitution of man is the work of nature; that of the state the work of art. It is not in men's power to prolong their own lives; but it is for them to prolong as much as possible the life of the State, by giving it the best possible constitution.

(Rousseau 1973: 235)

As we have just seen, Paine avoids having to make this sharp distinction between art and nature when he describes his idea of representative government. For him the assumption governing his unchanging geometric model is that it is not a human invention at all, but a discovery of the immutable laws of creation. For him the body becomes sacred, but it is only representative government which can overcome the transitory body or even those dying generations.[5] In this rather extreme sense, Paine is both beneath and beyond the thinking of his Burkean contemporaries. Instead of allowing for the possibility of a symbolic image which is capable of being individual and general at the same time in a mystery of representation, Paine moves from material object to invisible principle, and there is no accounting for the transference; there is no obscure aesthetic exchange, the kind of transubstantiation Coleridge might argue for.

In propounding an idea of imagination as part of a divisive world of human contrivance and muddled, inconsistent plurality, Paine's philosophy grounds itself in two ideas representing a unity which makes any aesthetic category look redundant. In one the system of representation is idyllic in that it contains no sense of difference. In the other we have a typical response to that which is supposed to stand resolutely outside it – the body. It figures as natural object. As a solution this too is fraught with problems, for it raises perhaps the most fundamental issue of Paine's period in the political sphere and the one which most closely bears on popular notions of imagination in the literature of the period – whether, in the form of sympathy or projection, it constitutes an act of knowledge which is capable of judging social realities. The tyranny of the individual represented by monarchy is to be replaced by the confinement of the body: in terms of representation, the symbolic individual is to be replaced by one which is supposed to stand outside the signifying chain altogether. When Paine develops his description of the representative form of government in *Rights of Man*, it inevitably leads to a language which is no language at all:

> Like the nation itself, it possesses a perpetual stamina, as well of body as of mind; and presents itself on the open theatre of the world in a fair and manly manner. Whatever are its excellences or its defects, they are visible to all. It exists not in fraud and mystery; it deals not in cant and sophistry, but inspires a language, that passing from heart to heart, is felt and understood.

> (Paine 1982: 204)

Ultimately, Paine's literalist mistrust of language and artifice, like many others, turns out to be grounded in a kind of fundamentalism. The apparently egalitarian openness of this passage is coupled with an organic vision of the body politic and an accession to commonsense ideology. Paine's radical literalism offers rational demystification alongside intuitive, affective truth. As such it is as likely to be appropriated by the rationalist Left as it is by the 'born-again' Right.

Notes

1. For recent studies of Paine dealing with the representation of revolution, the construction of audiences, and the role of language in the revolution controversy of the 1790s see Paulson, Ronald (1983). *Representations of Revolution*. New Haven and London, Yale University Press, esp. pp. 73–79; Klancher, Jon P. (1987). *The Making of English Reading Audiences, 1790–1832*. Madison, University of Wisconsin Press, esp. pp. 18–46; Smith, Olivia (1984). *The Politics of Language 1791–1819*. Oxford, Clarendon Press, esp. pp. 35–68. For the Anglo-American context of Paine's thought see Wilson, David A. (1988). *Paine and Cobbett: The Transatlantic Connection*. Kingston and Montreal, McGill-Queen's University Press.
2. See UEA English Studies group, 'Strategies for Representing Revolution' in Barker, Francis et al. (ed.) (1982). *1789: Reading, Writing Revolution*. Colchester, University of Essex, pp. 87–91.
3. See, for example, the following distinction: 'a scene so new, and so transcendentally unequalled by anything in the European world, that the name of Revolution is diminutive of its character, and it rises into a Regeneration.' (Paine 1982: 136).
4. See (Paine 1969: iii 404): 'Letters Addressed to American Citizens': 'The boldness . . . with which I speak on any subject, is a compliment to the judgement of the reader. It is like saying to him, I TREAT YOU AS A MAN AND NOT AS A CHILD.'
5. For an extended example of Paine's deployment of the body analogy see 'Decline and Fall of the English System of Finance', (Paine 1969: iii 286–312).

References

Paine, Thomas (1969, originally 1902). *The Writings of Thomas Paine* (ed.), Moncure, Daniel Conway. New York, Burt Franklin.

Paine, Thomas (1973). *Common Sense and the Crisis*. New York, Anchor Press.

Paine, Thomas (1982). *Rights of Man*. Harmondsworth, Penguin.

Rousseau, Jean-Jacques (1973). *The Social Contract and Discourses* (trans.), G.D.H. Cole. London, Dent.

Watson, Richard (1984) *Apology for the Bible in a Series of Letters Addressed to Thomas Paine* (8th edition, London 1797), in *William Blake's Annotations to Richard Watson's An Apology for the Bible in a Series of Letters Addressed to Thomas Paine* (ed.), James G. Ingli (1984). *Regency Reprints*. Cardiff, University of Wales Press.

7

Shelley, *The Cenci* and the French Revolution

Michael Rossington

Judge. Art thou not guilty of thy father's death?
Beatrice. Or wilt thou rather tax high judging God
That he permitted such an act as that
Which I have suffered, and which he beheld;
Made it unutterable, and took from it
All refuge, all revenge, all consequence,
But that which thou hast called my father's death?
Which is or is not what men call a crime,
Which either I have done, or have not done;
Say what ye will. I shall deny no more.
If ye desire it thus, thus let it be,
And so an end of all. Now do your will;
No other pains shall force another word.
(The Cenci, V, iii, 77–89)[1]

Andrew Webster

I

The Cenci addresses a question common to the most significant of Shelley's writings composed in the spring and summer of 1819, which include 'Julian and Maddalo' and the second and third acts of *Prometheus Unbound*: under what circumstances, and at what price, is the overthrow of tyranny possible?[2] *The Cenci* is the clearest indication that Shelley thought that history provided few examples of an individual overcoming tyrannical power successfully without succumbing to its corrupting influence. Such corruption of idealism and innocence occurs also, although in a different form, in 'Julian and Maddalo' where the price of the optimistic faith which Julian defends is symbolised by the solitary imprisonment of the maniac. Only *Prometheus Unbound* testifies to the possibility of transcending these localised, domestic histories through a universal myth in which the boundaries of history can be stretched to accommodate the revolutionary dimensions of 'beautiful idealisms of moral excellence' (Preface to *Prometheus Unbound*, Reiman and Powers 1977: 135).

The clear parallels between the two dramas in the tyrannical father figures, Jupiter and Cenci, and their curses, and the defiance of Prometheus and Beatrice, are less significant than the opposite outcomes which they relate, as well as the fact that they are clearly separated by different circumstances of composition and written for distinct audiences.[3] In *Prometheus Unbound*, the successful revolution depends on Prometheus's ability to refuse the satisfaction of violent revenge and thereby deny heroic selfhood; in *The Cenci*, Beatrice, faced with institutional coercion in the name of justice, finds that her father's sadistic, sexual crimes, as well as the murder referred to by Camillo in the first line of the play, can be appeased by the Church, while the punishment for others, like parricide, which threaten the state, knows no bounds. Beatrice's exemplary ruin lies not simply in the fact that her actions are not morally justifiable in Shelley's terms, let alone those of the savage Christian culture of the Italian Renaissance, but in the circumstantial necessity which appears to her to determine them. In short, the play sets the individual against institutional power; Beatrice's mythological and literary antecedence is closer to Antigone than Prometheus, in her challenge to political authority and in her loyalty to her brothers. Shelley's most powerful addition to Sophocles' drama is the parallel he draws between political and sexual oppression.

Much of the best criticism of *The Cenci* has taken what Shelley termed its 'sad reality' (Reiman and Powers 1977: 237) to refer to Beatrice's moral failure while acknowledging her fortitude as a tragic heroine (see Baker 1948: 138–153; Curran 1970: esp. 129–154; Curran 1975: 120–136; Wasserman 1971: 84–128; Deane 1988: 123–127; Sperry 1988: 127–142). Yet the moral issue of the play, centring on Beatrice's attempt to exculpate herself from the murder of her father, can also be interpreted as part of Shelley's critique of the French Revolution, and implicitly of the historical consequences of all revolutionary violence. Ronald Paulson has argued that '*The Cenci* . . . shows the way the actual revolution in France evolved – that is, the wrong way' (Paulson 1983: 281), and sees in the play 'the Burkean-Blakean assumption about the inevitable corruption of the revolution . . . the leveling to undifferentiation of the revolutionaries and the tyrants' (Paulson 1983: 281). For him, Beatrice is 'the key to the failure of the patricide-revolution. . . . By accepting the doctrine of paternal authority while killing the father, she merely becomes her father, assuming his own standards, laws, and religious superstition' (Paulson 1983: 281–2). Paulson also sees her impatient action as symptomatic of the reason why the Romantic poets despaired at the French Revolution:

> it will lead to the Terror . . . and Napoleonic imperialism . . . [and] to the 'gloom and misanthropy' of the succeeding age, to the mistaken retreat by the Wordsworths and Southeys from hopes of radical reform into conservative reaction, and to the 'infectious gloom' of Byron (Maddalo).
>
> (Paulson 1983: 282)

To see Beatrice's behaviour as an allegory of the failure of the French Revolution, however, is to see her as the sole agent of the perpetuation of tyranny in history, to give her a responsibility for evil in the play which underestimates the comparative strength of institutional power. All Shelley's poems about revolutionary politics, especially *Prometheus Unbound*, address the paradoxical replication of the relationship between master and slave, tyrant and victim, but *The Cenci* carefully avoids the idealism in his other dramatisations of historical change. For Beatrice's murder of her father is prompted by the specific, grotesque act of incestuous rape which is so literally unspeakable that redress cannot be sought from those judicial and religious authorities which had already overlooked other excesses of Cenci's domestic tyranny.

Although, in Shelley's eyes, this does not mitigate her crime, the consolidation of tyrannical power and its retribution which she unleashes is not something which she could have anticipated. There is no comfortable relationship between morality and history. In this sense, Shelley's allegory of the French Revolution in *The Cenci* does not, as Paulson implies, take the form simply of portraying its demise, and thereby dismissing revolutionary politics *per se*, as the earlier generation of Romantic poets had done. Shelley returns rather to the moment of revolutionary crisis itself which cannot, either in the domestic politics of *The Cenci* or the French Revolution itself, be pure of evil or self-interest. Nor are historical consequences predictable. Just as the French Revolution did not possess an internal logic, so Beatrice is not aware of the wider consequences of her action until she understands how hopeless it has been. Shelley reacted to first receiving news of Peterloo by quoting Beatrice's resolution to act after being raped by her father:

> The same day that your letter came, came the news of the Manchester work, & the torrent of my indignation has not yet done boiling in my veins. I wait anxiously [to] hear how the Country will express its sense of this bloody murderous oppression of its destroyers. 'Something must be done. . . . What yet I know not.' [*The Cenci*, III, i, 86–87]
>   (L513, To Charles Ollier, 6 Sept. 1819, Jones 1964: ii 117)

Yet Beatrice's words also reveal the fundamental scepticism in Shelley's own mind about being able to find an action commensurate with the crime performed in each case, a historical solution that would be prophetic of its consequences, or self-knowing. That Shelley's response to Peterloo was the passive resistance advocated in 'The Mask of Anarchy' indicates how far he was prepared to use a popular, self-consciously theatrical genre to propound a doctrine that in the localised situation of domestic politics, like that of *The Cenci*, he knew to be impossible to sustain.

Instead of seeing it simply as a negative critique of the morality of revolution, this essay proposes to examine the play's force as a dramatisation of the teleology of the suffering under, and resistance to, tyranny that lead to its paradoxical reinforcement and perpetuation. Beatrice represents not simply the legacy of the specific historical tragedy which haunted Shelley, the thwarting of revolutionary possibility (this fear was the main bequest of what was perceived by him to be the failure of the

French Revolution) but the blindness to historical consequences which the individual suffers in seeking to redress evil. *The Cenci* can be seen, then, in the context of Shelley's perception of historical development in which revolution is always necessary yet necessarily blind to its own destiny.

II

While *The Cenci* represents the culmination of an effort to explain the consequences of revolution for the individual, it also develops two influences on Shelley's wider theory of historical development evident in his early work, the Enlightenment concept of Necessity and the Manichaean model of a universe governed by good and evil spirits successively, which Shelley gleaned, under the influence of Peacock, from Zoroastrian mythology (see Curran 1975: 119–152 and Butler 1983). In *Queen Mab*, revolution is an impersonal agent of historical change through which Necessity guarantees the impermanence of tyranny, as it does in Volney's *Ruins of Empires*. Like Volney, Shelley confidently telescopes history, including that of a contemporary, imperial variety symbolised by Napoleon, into a series of vain illusions of grandeur. In the materialist tradition of French Enlightenment thought as adapted by Volney and Godwin, Necessity connotes progressive change, but in their zeal to eschew a millenarian historical vision associated with Christian prophecy, instability appears a condition of such progress. The question of how a desirable political order can ever be incorporated permanently into such a historical scheme is deferred.

After the end of the Napoleonic war, when ostentatious imperial ambition had been curtailed, Necessity alone seems too unstable a category to provide assurance about the political future of Europe. The destructive activity of the glaciers in 'Mont Blanc' can only offer a tentative analogy to the desired course of history. With the death of Napoleon, the French Revolution now assumes a historical identity as 'the master theme of the epoch in which we live' (L361, To Lord Byron, 8 Sept. 1816, Jones 1964: i, 504), which is suitable for epic treatment as 'involving pictures of all that is best qualified to interest and to instruct mankind' (L363, To Lord Byron, 29 Sept. 1816, Jones 1964: i, 508). In *Laon and Cythna; or, The Revolution of the Golden City: A Vision of The Nineteenth Century*, his most explicit allegory of the French Revolution and its consequences, Shelley uses a mythological model to suggest how the defeat of revolutionary hope can be redressed. By exploiting the Manichaean emphasis on the dualism of good and evil in Zoroastrian mythology which resolves itself in terms of the alternate reigns of Ormusd and Ahriman, the impermanence of an ultimately desirable political order remains unresolved but a paradoxical security is gained from the knowledge that a reign of evil and despair will be succeeded by one of good and hope. *Laon and Cythna* anatomises the psychology of revolution and the despair of its failure while also offering to transcend it.

Shelley's verdict on how the French Revolution failed in the Preface to *Laon and Cythna* is important to that circumstantial necessity or teleology which Beatrice both conducts, and is conducted by, in *The Cenci*:

> It has ceased to be believed that whole generations of mankind ought to consign themselves to a hopeless inherit- ance of ignorance and misery, because a nation of men who had been dupes and slaves for centuries were incapable of conducting themselves with the wisdom and tranquillity of freemen so soon as some of their fetters were partially loosened. That their conduct could not have been marked by any other characters than ferocity and thoughtlessness is the historical fact from which liberty derives all its recom- mendations, and falsehood the worst features of its de- formity.
>
> (Clark 1988: 316)

The 'historical fact' of this inevitable failure must then be seen as a recommendation for freedom, not for the deforming powers of despair. Shelley's singular acknowledgement of the French Revolution's failure becomes a hallmark of all his subsequent treatments of revolution which insist on the paradox of deriving sustenance from the destruction of those heroes and heroines like Laon and Cythna who resist tyranny. Rape, revenge or sacrifice are suffered by the protagonists, Cythna, Beatrice, Laon and Prometheus with relentless violence. They become symbols of a compulsion to acknowledge defeat which only imaginative effort can overcome. For Shelley political hope can only be founded on an acknowledgement of the destruction or sacrifice of those who resist.

Moreover, in an illuminating comment of relevance to *The Cenci*, Shelley notes that at the root of the failure of the French

Revolution was 'a defect of correspondence between the knowledge existing in society and the improvement or gradual abolition of political institutions' (Clark 1988: 316). This confidence that the Revolution manifested 'a general state of feeling amongst civilised mankind' (Clark 1988: 316) which was not in itself culpable but simply unworkable because the relationship between knowledge and political institutions was disjoined, suggests a theory of history based upon a wholly attainable ideal historical moment in which institutions will reflect the degree of enlightened knowledge in a society, and thereby become, in a Godwinian sense, obsolete. But *Laon and Cythna* represents exemplary individuals of the romance genre in whom private and public, love and politics are fused unproblematically, 'little else than visions which impersonate my own apprehensions of the beautiful and the just' (Reiman and Powers 1977: 237), as he described his previous works in the Dedication to *The Cenci*. *The Cenci* represents the ruthless separation of public from private, of domestic politics from society, to a degree that paralyses the individual and sanctions self-interest.

Ultimately Shelley takes refuge, especially after the revolutions in southern Europe in 1820, in accommodating the French Revolution into a republican tradition beginning with classical Athens. This is implicit in the optimistic schemas of both 'Ode to Liberty' and *Hellas*. The earlier dualism, influenced by Zoroastrianism, is replaced by a tradition which can acknowledge the failure of revolutions as part of a series of eventually victorious symbols. This is much closer in fact, to Shelley's sense of the poet and of poetry itself in *A Defence of Poetry*, as being forever sacrificed to the interests of a radical future.

III

Shelley's play was conceived as a 'popular' work for immediate performance which would appeal to a mass audience:

> It is written without any of the peculiar feelings & opinions which characterize my other compositions, I having attending [*for* attended] simply to the impartial development of such characters as it is probable the persons represented really were, together with the greatest degree of popular effect to be produced by such a development.
>
> (L504, To Thomas Love Peacock, [c.20] July 1819, Jones 1964: ii 102)

Since he felt that, '"Cenci" is written for the multitude, and ought to sell well' (L551, To Ollier, 6 March 1820, Jones 1964: ii 174), he reacted to its rejection by theatres with a mixture of modest self-deprecation and genuine bafflement. He later admitted that 'nothing is so difficult and unwelcome as to write without a confidence of finding readers; and if my play of "The Cenci" found none or few, I despair of ever producing anything that shall merit them' (L605, To Peacock, 15 Feb. 1820 [for 1821], Jones 1964: ii 262). The play is a response to Mary's encouragement to strive for an audience and a market which he had hitherto denied himself (see her 'Note on The Cenci', Hutchinson 1970: 334–337), and was 'studiously written in a style very different from any other [of my] compositions' (L560, To Thomas Jefferson Hogg, 20 April 1820, Jones 1964: ii, 186). Shelley sensed that he could achieve through drama a popularity and a political impact which his poetry had obscured.[4]

In his Preface, Shelley proclaims the universal, almost classical status of the play, through describing its origins in the folklore of Roman society: 'This national and universal interest which the story produces and has produced for two centuries and among all ranks of people in a great City . . . first suggested to me the conception of its fitness for a dramatic purpose' (Reiman and Powers 1977: 239). To use oral tradition in such a way was to make claims for literary credibility, but also to emphasize the roots of its authenticity in popular culture:

> Nothing remained as I imagined, but to clothe it to the appre-
> hensions of my countrymen in such language and action as
> would bring it home to their hearts. The deepest and sub-
> limest tragic compositions, *King Lear* and the two plays in
> which the tale of Œdipus is told, were stories which clearly
> existed in tradition, as matters of popular belief and interest,
> before Shakespeare and Sophocles made them familiar to the
> sympathy of all succeeding generations of mankind.
>
> (Reiman and Powers 1977: 239)

Such ambitious claims reveal the distinctive identity of the play, not as a mythological venture of his own but as a narrative rooted in a specific history, 'I lay aside the presumptuous attitude of the instructor, and am content to paint . . . that which has been' (Reiman and Powers 1977: 237). Yet the nature of these literary claims, and of his justification of his choice of the play, conceal his motive to use the play to challenge religious and political tyranny, at a point when radical fortunes in England were on the defensive.

His assurance to his publisher, Charles Ollier, that *The Cenci* has 'no reference, direct or indirect, to politics, or religion' (L519, To Ollier, 15 Oct. 1819, Jones 1964: ii, 127) was therefore a deceptive precaution to ensure that his anonymity was preserved while a theatre to perform the play was sought (see Cameron and Reiman 1961–86: vi, 929). It is contradicted by the force of the 'Dedication' to Leigh Hunt, published with the play:

> In that patient and irreconcileable enmity with domestic and political tyranny and imposture which the tenor of your life has illustrated, and which, had I health and talents should illustrate mine, let us, comforting each other in our task, live and die.
>
> (Reiman and Powers 1977: 238)[5]

In reviewing *The Cenci*, Hunt drew attention to the discrepancy between the manuscript source (transcribed by Mary in May 1818) which described Cenci as an atheist, and his nominal Catholicism in Shelley's play: 'the atheism of such men as Cenci is the only real atheism; that is to say, it is the only real disbelief in any great and good thing, physical or moral' (Hunt 1820b: 330, rpt. in Reiman 1972: Part C, ii 476)[6]. More contentiously Hunt argued that it was institutionalised Christianity which was responsible for, and therefore compatible with, Cenci's atheism:

> The vices of his atheism and the vices of his superstition would, in a spirit of his temper and education, have alike been the result of a pernicious system of religious faith, which rendered the Divine Being gross enough to be disbelieved by any one, and imitated and bribed by the wicked.
>
> (Hunt 1820b: 331, rpt. in Reiman 1972: Part C, ii 476)

The corruption of Christian ethics by the Church has been argued by Stuart Curran to be responsible for Beatrice's fall: 'Had Beatrice not been trained from childhood to weigh the comparative gradations of sins, she would have lacked authority for the casuistry by which she justifies her father's murder' (Curran 1975: 135). It should be remembered, however, that Shelley's drama does not forgive Beatrice in these terms.

The refusal to acknowledge a Christian ethic in which good will eventually prevail over evil shocked contemporary reviewers of

The Cenci. The Monthly Review noted that 'the principle of evil overcomes, for a long and weary time, the principle of good' (*The Monthly Review* 1821: 163, rpt. in Reiman 1972: Part C, ii 721) and went further with reference to *Prometheus Unbound*:

> His Manichean absurdities, his eternally indwelling notion of a good and an evil principle fighting like furies on all occasions with their whole *posse comitatus* together, cross his clearer fancy, and lay the buildings of his better mind in glittering gorgeous ruins.
>
> > (*The Monthly Review* 1821: 169, rpt. in Reiman 1972: Part C, ii 724)

This heresy is part of that exploration of Manicheaism which was argued earlier to underlie much of Shelley's mythological treatment of history and revolution, influenced by Zoroastrianism and most strongly developed in his satirical essay, 'On the Devil and Devils'.[7] But there were other, more immediate reasons for offence.

The reviewers reacted strongly to the exposition of incestuous rape and parricide which appeared to them to be gratuitous, 'In an evil hour does the pleasure of exhibiting might, first tempt the hand of genius to withdraw the veil from things that ought for ever to remain concealed . . .' (*Edinburgh Monthly Review* 1820: 592, rpt. in Reiman 1972: Part C, i 347). Such objections had been anticipated by Shelley. His principal doubt about its success as 'an acting play' centred on the question

> as to whether any such a thing as incest in this shape however treated wd. be admitted on the stage – I think however it will form no objection, considering first that the facts are matter of history, & secondly the peculiar delicacy with which I have treated it –
>
> > (L504, To Peacock, 20 July 1819, Jones 1964: ii 102)

Later he justifies its function in the play by appealing, as he had done in the Preface, to classical precedent: 'I do not see how the subject forms an objection. You know "Œdipus" is performed on the fastidious French stage, a play much more broad than this' (L514, To Peacock, 9 Sept. 1819, Jones 1964: ii 118–119). Incest, however, also had its political usages. The sexual love between brother and sister in the suppressed *Laon and Cythna* had not served as a 'matter of history' but as a dimension of the poem's radical intention whose significance many critics understood.

With reference to its previous incarnation, John Taylor Coleridge's review of *The Revolt of Islam* testified to Shelley's exposure of the extension of institutional tyranny into domestic political economy:

> He has indeed, to the best of his ability, wounded us in the tenderest part. – As far as in him lay, he has loosened the hold of our protecting laws, and sapped the principles of our venerable polity; he has invaded the purity and chilled the unsuspecting ardour of our fireside intimacies; he has slandered, ridiculed and blasphemed our holy religion . . .
> (Coleridge 1819: 469, rpt. in Reiman 1972, Part C, ii 775)

Shelley's strategic use of incest in *Laon and Cythna* to contribute to the subversion that Coleridge notes, is then entirely distinct from its symbolic corruption of domestic and social life in *The Cenci*. He later discusses the opposite literary uses of incest:

> Incest is like many other *incorrect* things a very poetical circumstance. It may be the excess of love or of hate. It may be that defiance of every thing for the sake of another which clothes itself in the glory of the highest heroism, or it may be that cynical rage which confounding the good & bad in existing opinions breaks through them for the purpose of rioting in selfishness & antipathy.
> (L531, To Maria Gisborne, 16 Nov. 1819, Jones 1964: ii 154)

That the reviews were often unable to distinguish between incest as a revolutionary act and, in the case of *The Cenci*, as the abuse of tyranny is indicative of how the radicalism of the play could be wilfully misread.

Shelley located the moral dilemma of the story in terms of its emotional currency in contemporary Italian society where it aroused towards Beatrice 'a romantic pity for the wrongs, and a passionate exculpation of the horrible deed to which they urged her' (Reiman and Powers 1977: 239). This recognition of an audience's potential sympathies contributes to his decision not to create a heroic figure, more like his Prometheus, who eschews revenge, but to remain faithful to the story as related in the manuscript. Promethean self-denial in his tragic heroine would have lacked credibility to a popular audience:

> Revenge, retaliation, atonement, are pernicious mistakes. If Beatrice had thought in this manner she would have been wiser and better; but she would never have been a tragic

character: the few whom such an exhibition would have interested, could never have been sufficiently interested for a dramatic purpose, from the want of finding sympathy in their interest among the mass who surround them.

(Reiman and Powers 1977: 240)

His directive for the play's performance, however, is that the moral outcome must not undermine its dramatic appeal, 'There must also be nothing attempted to make the exhibition subservient to what is vulgarly termed a moral purpose' (Reiman and Powers 1977: 240). The function of the play is to test the limits of moral judgement alone, by placing the onus of the play on her circumstances:

> It is in the restless and anatomizing casuistry with which men seek the justification of Beatrice, yet feel that she has done what needs justification; it is in the superstitious horror with which they contemplate alike her wrongs and their revenge; that the dramatic character of what she did and suffered, consists.

(Reiman and Powers 1977: 240)

This is the moral question to be addressed to all revolutionaries, both in France in the Revolution and in contemporary England.

The case against Beatrice is that she is not simply a victim but that, in the final act, she wilfully manipulates the destiny of others. Her chilling attempt to exculpate herself through intimidating the wretched assassin Marzio leads to him forgoing his accusation of her because, 'That stern yet piteous look, those solemn tones,/ Wound worse than torture' (V, ii, 109–110). Beatrice shows herself capable of an appalling casuistry to justify her actions at the cost of his life, and the logic of her justification involves an apparently devious presumption of divine will:

> so my hate
> Became the only worship I could lift
> To our great father, who in pity and love,
> Armed thee, as thou dost say, to cut him off;
> And thus his wrong becomes my accusation;
> And art thou the accuser? If thou hopest
> Mercy in heaven, shew justice upon earth:
> Worse than a bloody hand is a hard heart.
>
> (V, ii, 126–133)

By presenting her action as part of a necessity sanctioned by God, Marzio is made to accede willingly to his death:

> Torture me as ye will:
> A keener pain has wrung a higher truth
> From my last breath. She is most innocent!
> Bloodhounds, not men, glut yourselves well with me;
> I will not give you that fine piece of nature
> To rend and ruin.
>
> (V, ii, 163–168)

In the same scene Camillo, whose judgement is shown to be flawed throughout the play, remarks that 'She is as pure as speechless infancy!' (V, ii, 69). That these are tragically inappropriate terms in which to proclaim her innocence, for she is now no longer 'a fine piece of nature' but is truly corrupted, and her language bears no semblance to 'speechless infancy', is part of Shelley's dramatic irony, which is compounded when the instrument of justice, Savella, arrives too late to take the action against Cenci that Beatrice inflicts through revenge. Her own sense of necessity which operates for her through Marzio is undermined by the arbitrary intervention of that necessity which leads to her death.

Yet necessity is also shown to be unaccommodating. While Beatrice herself is seen by Shelley as its victim, 'violently thwarted from her nature by the necessity of circumstance and opinion' (Reiman and Powers 1977: 238), other characters are compelled by its ironies. For Giacomo, 'still doubting if that deed/ Be just which is most necessary' (III, ii, 7–8), and for Lucretia hearing the warrant for Cenci's death after the murder, 'All was prepared by unforbidden means/ Which we must pay so dearly, having done' (IV, iv, 29–30), necessity is in conflict with morality. For Beatrice, it is always possible to win necessity round to one's viewpoint, as she confidently asserts at the end of the fourth act, after Lucretia has fainted:

> She cannot know how well the supine slaves
> Of blind authority read the truth of things
> When written on a brow of guilelessness:
> She sees not yet triumphant Innocence
> Stand at the judgement-seat of mortal man,
> A judge and an accuser of the wrong
> Which drags it there.
>
> (IV, iv, 181–187)

The bitter irony of these lines is something she learns by the end of the play when she refuses all hope:

> Worse than despair,
> Worse than the bitterness of death, is hope:
> It is the only ill which can find place
> Upon the giddy, sharp and narrow hour
> Tottering beneath us.
>
> (V, iv, 97–101)

When necessity fails to coincide with her own moral instinct for justice, Beatrice seeks the certainty of total destruction, the negation of the future, and submission to a perverted necessity which is preferable to the possibility of redemption. This is the fate of revolutionary idealism which submits to historical necessity instead of fashioning another kind of necessity anew.

However reprehensible her display of cruelty and self-deception, Beatrice has the power to anatomise the consequences of oppression and tyranny, in a way that the other victims, including Giacomo, racked by guilt and indecision, cannot:

> My pangs are of the mind, and of the heart,
> And of the soul; aye, of the inmost soul,
> Which weeps within tears as of burning gall
> To see, in this ill world where none are true,
> My kindred false to their deserted selves.
> And with considering all the wretched life
> Which I have lived, and its now wretched end,
> And the small justice shown by Heaven and Earth
> To me or mine; and what a tyrant thou art,
> And what slaves these; and what a world we make,
> The oppressor and the oppressed . . .
>
> (V, iii, 65–76)

This diagnosis of the replication of the master-slave relationship, so important to Shelley's understanding of revolution, indicates Beatrice's apprehension of the momentous legacy of her action. Yet this clear-sighted detachment is more than clinical. In her final speeches, after the court scene, Beatrice transcends self-justification, questioning the very foundation of a world in which she can have no recourse to justice. Most important, and consistent with her own loss of faith, is the integrity of her refusal to accept any comfort from religion. Her piety to Lucretia that God 'Seems, and but seems to have abandoned us' (V, iii, 115), is converted, when she hears that the Pope has refused to grant a pardon of the death penalty, into a lucid speculation on the arbitrariness of religious faith:

> If there should be
> No God, no Heaven, no Earth in the void world;
> The wide, grey, lampless, deep, unpeopled world!
> If all things then should be . . . my father's spirit,
> His eye, his voice, his touch surrounding me;
> The atmosphere and breath of my dead life!
>
> (V, iv, 57–62)[8]

In fact the only powerful presence she can conceive of governing the universe in the after-life is her father, 'For was he not alone omnipotent/ On Earth, and ever present?' (V, iv, 68–69). No morality has operated with justice towards her, 'No difference has been made by God or man,/ Or any power moulding my wretched lot,/ 'Twixt good or evil, as regarded me' (V, iv, 82–84), and she has no faith that the course of history will be altered by man except by destruction of that very bond with her siblings which she, and Antigone, had sought to preserve, 'Cruel, cold, formal man; righteous in words,/ In deeds a Cain' (V, iv, 108–109).

This inability to reconcile her private suffering with the morality of the political order emphasizes the parallel between Beatrice and Antigone, the classical heroine who symbolises the need to resist the violation and brutality of public law and, in a comparable sense to the French revolutionaries, the need to use brotherly and sisterly love as a means of opposing tyrannical parents. In an early letter to Hogg, just after his expulsion from Oxford, Shelley had chosen Antigone to exemplify the incompatibility of personal ethics and political rule:

> but is the Antigone immoral. Did she wrong when she acted in direct in noble violation of the laws of a prejudiced society. You will I know have the candor to acknowledge that yr. premise will not stand & I now most perfectly agree with you that political affairs are quite distinct from morality, that they cannot be united –
>
> (L68, To Thomas Jefferson Hogg, 9 May 1811,
> Jones 1964: i 81–82)

That a political system engaged in forging a new morality could itself be corrupted was one of the ironic lessons of the French Revolution, but the point for Shelley here is that Antigone, like Beatrice, refuses acquiescence to a corrupt order and hence cannot be dismissed simply as immoral. Later Antigone is a model of that Shelleyan category of ideal, revolutionary womanhood:

> You are right about Antigone – how sublime a picture of a woman! And what think you of the chorus's, & especially the lyrical complaints of the godlike victim? – and the menaces of Tiresias & their rapid fulfilment? Some of us have in a prior existence been in love with an Antigone, & that makes us find no full content in any mortal tie.
>
> (L668, To John Gisborne, 22 Oct. 1821, Jones 1964: ii 364)

Like Antigone, Beatrice is a victim of a brutality that is envisaged prophetically in terms of Peterloo: 'Oh! He has trampled me/ Under his feet, and made the blood stream down/ My pallid cheeks.' (II, i, 64–66)[9]

The Church represents the institutional oppression, noted in both the Preface to *Laon and Cythna* and *A Philosophical View of Reform*, which prevents political change from occurring peacefully and induces revenge and punishment in any revolutionary situation. The Pope, cited by Camillo, perceives his impartiality towards Cenci's actions as a means of preserving his authority from being undermined by the young:

> 'Children are disobedient, and they sting
> Their fathers' hearts to madness and despair
> Requiting years of care with contumely . . .
> In the great war between old and young
> I, who have white hairs and a tottering body,
> Will keep at least blameless neutrality.'
>
> (II, ii, 32–34, 38–40)

The Pope's defensive words, always delivered indirectly by Camillo, appear to derive from an oracular source, making him an inverted mirror-image of Demogorgon in *Prometheus Unbound*. His neurotic fear of parricide is an exemplary form of resistance to change:

> 'Parricide grows so rife
> That soon, for some just cause no doubt, the young
> Will strangle us all, dozing in our chairs.
> Authority, and power, and hoary hair
> Are grown crimes capital.'
>
> (V, iv, 20–24)

This paranoid fantasy of a patriarchal society being devoured by its young heightens the Burkean vision of the self-consuming

monster of cyclical destruction associated with the French
Revolution. The Pope's indifference to suffering, 'a marble form,/
A rite, a law, a custom: not a man' (V, iv, 4–5), suggests that he is
the primary instrument of that cruel inversion of humanity which
Beatrice comes to see at the end of the play as reality.

In *The Cenci*, there is no language for an alternative to this
corrupt morality, just as there is no language for the maniac's
'incommunicable woe' ('Julian and Maddalo', 343), nor for
Prometheus's suffering in Act I of *Prometheus Unbound*. The
condition of tyranny is that it silences the oppressed (see Worton
1982). Beatrice cannot articulate the violation of her body and
spirit, 'If I try to speak/ I shall go mad. Aye, something must be
done;/ What, yet I know not . . . something which shall make/
The thing that I have suffered but a shadow/ In the dread
lightning which avenges it' (III, i, 86–89). This lack of a vocabulary
to repeal injustice reinforces the impossible divide between
private suffering and public morality, as Lucretia realises:

> But if one, like this wretch,
> Should mock, with gold, opinion, law and power?
> If there be no appeal to that which makes
> The guiltiest tremble? If because our wrongs,
> For that they are, unnatural, strange and monstrous,
> Exceed all measure of belief? O God!
> If, for the very reasons which should make
> Redress most swift and sure, our injurer triumphs?
> And we the victims, bear worse punishment
> Than that appointed for their torturer?
>
> (III, i, 184–193)

These 'monstrous' wrongs yield their own progeny, and the
word, with its echoes of the deformed revolution of the 1790s, is
used by the judge to taunt the culprits of 'this monstrous crime'
(V, ii, 72). In Beatrice's fear of the legacy of her family to posterity,
'Infamy, blood, terror, despair' (V, iii, 45), lies the image of the
French Revolution inherited by Shelley's generation. Yet, at the
heart of the play is the more radical message that the true
revolution remains unaccomplished, deflected from its path by
the negating powers of religion and patriarchy. For Beatrice it is
'high judging God' (V, iii, 78) that made her rape 'unutterable,
and took from it/ All refuge, all revenge, all consequence/ But that
which thou hast called my father's death[?]' (V, iii, 81–83). The

bequest of the French Revolution and of the revolutions Shelley prophesied in his own day was a distortion of the vocabulary in which resistance could be articulated. Beatrice's tragic awareness of this elevates her above the despair and misanthropy which Shelley attacked in the Preface to *Laon and Cythna*. Yet she remains within the tangible context of a historical version of oppression recognisable to his projected popular audience, and far removed from the other-worldly idealism of the visionary revolution of *Prometheus Unbound*.

Notes

1. Unless stated otherwise, all references to *The Cenci* are to the text in Reiman and Powers 1977, which is based on the first edition, as corrected from the errata leaf in the possession of Mary Shelley. All other references to Shelley's poems are also to Reiman and Powers 1977.
2. For the order of composition of these works, see Matthews and Everest 1989: xxxvii.
3. For the circumstances of composition of *The Cenci* at Rome and at Villa Valsovano, see Holmes 1976: 509–528.
4. For the influence of Schlegel 1815 on Shelley's conception of drama as a social form, see Tetreault 1987: 122–128. The dramatic and political strategy of *The Cenci* in engaging the audience's sympathies is discussed in Behrendt 1989: 144–160.
5. For the manuscipt of the draft of the 'Dedication', which is more aggressive in its political sentiments than the published version, see SC532 in Cameron and Reiman 1961–86: vi, 865–874.
6. For the text of the 'Relation of the Death of the Family of the Cenci', see Buxton Forman 1880: ii, 399–417. For a brief history of the manuscript of the 'Relation' see Cameron and Reiman 1961–86: vi, 897–898.
7. For an argument for dating 'On the Devil and Devils' in 1820 see Butler 1989; for dating in 1819, see Curran and Wittreich 1972.
8. In V, iv, 60, I have followed the second edition of *The Cenci* (Shelley 1821) which has a comma after 'spirit'; there is no comma in Reiman and Powers 1977, the copy-text for which is Shelley 1819.
9. The parallel with Sophocles' play is also present in Cenci's curse: 'and when dead/ As she shall die unshrived and unforgiven,/ A rebel to her father and her God,/ Her corpse shall be abandoned to the hounds' (IV, i, 88–91).

References

Baker, C. (1948). *Shelley's Major Poetry: The Fabric of A Vision*. Princeton, Princeton University Press.

Behrendt, S. C. (1989). *Shelley and His Audiences*. Lincoln, University of Nebraska Press.

Butler, M.S. (1983). 'Myth and Mythmaking in the Shelley Circle' in *Shelley Revalued: Essays from the Gregynog Conference*, ed. K. Everest. Leicester, Leicester University Press, 1–19.

—— (1989). 'Romantic Manichaeism: Shelley's "On the Devil and Devils" and Byron's Mythological Dramas' in *The Sun is God: Painting, Literature and Mythology in the Nineteenth Century*, ed. J.B. Bullen. Oxford, Clarendon Press, 13–37.

Cameron, K.N. and D.H. Reiman, eds. (1961–86). *Shelley and His Circle, 1773–1822*. 8 vols. to date. Vols. i–iv, ed. Cameron, vols. v–viii, ed. Reiman. Cambridge, Mass., Harvard University Press.

Clark, D.L., ed. (1988). *Shelley's Prose: The Trumpet of a Prophecy*. Ed. D.L. Clark, new edition. London, Fourth Estate (first published 1954, corrected edition 1966).

Coleridge, J.T. (1819). Review of *Laon and Cythna* and *The Revolt of Islam, Quarterly Review* 21, April 1819, 460–471, rpt. in Reiman, Part C, ii, 770–776.

Curran, S. (1970). *Shelley's Cenci: Scorpions Ringed with Fire*. Princeton, Princeton University Press.

—— (1975). *Shelley's Annus Mirabilis: The Maturing of an Epic Vision*. San Marino, Ca., Huntington Library.

Curran, S. and J. Wittreich Jr. (1972). 'The Dating of Shelley's "On the Devil and Devils"', *KSJ*, 21, 83–94.

Deane, S. (1988). *The French Revolution and the Enlightenment in England, 1789–1832*. Cambridge, Mass., Harvard University Press.

Edinburgh Monthly Review (1820). Review of *The Cenci, Edinburgh Monthly Review* 3 (May 1820), 591–604, rpt. in Reiman, Part C, i, 346–352.

Forman, H.B., ed. (1880). *The Works of Percy Bysshe Shelley in Verse and Prose*. 8 vols. London, Reeves and Turner.

Holmes, R. (1976). *Shelley: The Pursuit*. London, Quartet Books.

Hunt, L. (1820a). 'The Destruction of the Cenci family, and Tragedy on that subject', *The Indicator*, 51, 19 July 1820, 321–328, rpt. in Reiman, Part C, ii, 471–475.

—— (1820b). 'The Destruction of the Cenci family, and Tragedy on that Subject', *The Indicator*, 52, 26 July 1820, 329–336, rpt. in Reiman, Part C, ii, 475–479.

Hutchinson, T., ed. (1970). *Shelley: Poetical Works* (1905). 2nd ed. corrected by G. M. Matthews. Oxford, Oxford University Press.

Jones, F.L., ed. (1964). *The Letters of Percy Bysshe Shelley*. 2 vols. Oxford, Clarendon Press.

Matthews, G.M. and K. Everest, eds. (1989). *The Poems of Shelley*, vol. 1, 1804–17. London, Longman.

The Monthly Review (1821). Review of *The Cenci, The Monthly Review*, 2nd series, 94 (Feb. 1821), 161–168, rpt. in Reiman, Part C, ii, 720–723.

Paulson, R. (1983). *Representations of Revolution (1789–1820)*. New Haven, Conn., Yale University Press.

Reiman, D.H., ed. (1972). *The Romantics Reviewed: Contemporary Reviews of British Romantic Writers*. 3 parts. 9 vols. New York, Garland.

Reiman, D.H. and S.B. Powers, eds. (1977). *Shelley's Poetry and Prose*. New York, Norton.

Schlegel, A.W. (1815). *A Course of Lectures on Dramatic Art and Literature*. Trans. John Black. 2 vols. London, Baldwin, Cradock and Joy (first published in German, 1809–11).

Shelley, P. B. (1819). *The Cenci. A Tragedy. In Five Acts*. London, C. and J. Ollier.

Shelley, P. B. (1819). *The Cenci. A Tragedy. In Five Acts*. London, C. and J. Ollier.

—— (1821). *The Cenci. A Tragedy. In Five Acts*, 2nd edition. London, C. and J. Ollier.

Sperry, S.M. (1988). *Shelley's Major Verse: The Narrative and Dramatic Poetry*. Cambridge, Mass., Harvard University Press.

Tetreault, R. (1987). *The Poetry of Life: Shelley and Literary Form*. Toronto, University of Toronto Press.

Wasserman, E. (1971). *Shelley: A Critical Reading*. Baltimore, Johns Hopkins University Press.

Worton, M. (1982). 'Speech and Silence in *The Cenci*', in *Essays on Shelley*, ed. Miriam Allott. Liverpool, Liverpool University Press, 105–124.

Andrew Webster

Index